UNDER HER
Wings

UNDER HER
Wings

Spiritual Guidance from Women Saints

KATHY BENCE

UPPER
ROOM BOOKS®
NASHVILLE

Cover design: Thelma Whitworth
Cover art: Illustration of Julian of Norwich © Robert Lentz, 1995
    (Icons by Robert Lentz are available from Trinity Stores, 1-800-699-4482.)
Interior design: Ed Maksimowicz
Second printing: 2002

See page 224 for an extension of this copyright page.

Library of Congress Cataloging-in-Publication Data
Bence, Kathy, 1951–
    Under her wings : spiritual guidance from women saints / by Kathy Bence.
    p. cm.
    Includes bibliographical references.
    ISBN 0-8358-0943-9
    1. Christian women saints—Biography. 2. Christian women—Religious life.
    3. Spiritual life. I. Title.
282'.092'2—dc21
[B]   2001017376

To Jill,
a living saint,
who introduced me
to the depths

Contents

Women of Substance

*I*grew up in a Methodist family in Kentucky, lived a normal, rural
life in the 1950s, and never realized how limited my knowledge of
Christendom was. I felt called to ministry at age twelve and graduated
from a Christian college and seminary. During the 1980s, my husband
and I lived in Scotland for three years. While we were there, I discovered the wealth of centuries of the saints' writing. I remember saying
to my husband, Phil, "Why has no one ever told me about them?" I
devoured their writings hungrily. They became companions on my
spiritual journey.

Why would I want to write about women with eccentric habits who
lived hundreds of years ago? Because they fascinate me. Their personal lives are so foreign to mine. But more than that, they inspire and
serve as spiritual models for me—almost like mother figures.

These five women became my spiritual directors as I researched
their lives and read their writings. A spiritual director helps discern
God's presence in your life situations. As my spiritual directors, these
women rekindled a flame in me as I read of their fiery passion for God.
Through their self-renunciation they gently trained and rebuked me.
And then they invited me onward—closer to becoming the passionate
seeker of God I long to be. I know that their advice will bring out the
best in me—if I will apply it to my life.

Absorbing the writings of these women made me want to share
their wisdom and insights with others. I offer them to you as a gift that
is best enjoyed slowly and reflectively.

I suggest getting a cup of tea, a journal, and a Bible to use as companions to this book of fifty readings. You may spend several days with
a day's selection and/or skip readings that do not apply to your current
spiritual state. For each reading I have presented a brief excerpt of that
saint's writings, my musings on the excerpt, questions for reflection,
related scriptures (you may read all the suggested passages or as many

as you have time for), and an exercise to help you apply the truths you glean. I hope that you will make this book your own. Get to know each woman and learn all you can from her. In case you get hooked on any of these saints, see "Suggested Reading," page 218.

When I discussed with my husband how to approach this book, he came up with the title *Under Her Wings*. I love this title because it conveys the idea of protection and guidance from someone who's bigger and more experienced—a mother hen-and-chick image.

That is exactly how I felt as I read the writings of these five women saints and studied their lives—I have lived under their wings of experience of God. They have sheltered me and carried me closer to God when I feared proceeding alone. They have lived in the depths of God, while I have merely paddled in the shallows. Their example has inspired me to launch out into the depths, and that is my prayer for each of you.

Notes on the Text

 ℰach day's selection begins with an excerpt from the writings of one of the women who are the focus of this book. The language and style of writing reflect the historical period in which each saint lived and will require careful reading.

I like what Keith Beasley-Topliffe says about approaching spiritual classics:

> Reading spiritual classics is different from most of the reading we do. We have learned to read to master a text and extract information from it. We tend to read quickly, to get through a text. And we summarize as we read, seeking the main point. In reading spiritual classics, though, we allow the text to master and form us. Such formative reading goes more slowly, more reflectively, allowing time for God to speak to us through the text. God's word for us may come as easily from a minor point or even an aside as from the major point.
>
> Formative reading requires that you approach the text in humility. Read as a seeker, not an expert. . . . Humility means accepting the author as another imperfect human, a product of his or her own time and situation. Learn to celebrate what is foundational in an author's writing without being overly disturbed by what is peculiar to the author's life and times. Trust the text as a gift from both God and the author, offered to you for your benefit—to help you grow in Christ.
>
> To read formatively, you must also slow down. . . . Stop from time to time to reflect on what you have been reading. Keep a journal for these reflections. Often the act of writing can itself prompt further, deeper reflection. Keep your notebook open and your pencil in hand as you read. You might not get back to that wonderful insight later.[1]

Where possible and when the copyright holder granted permission, excerpts were edited for inclusive language and to conform scripture quotations to the New Revised Standard Version.

In speaking of the soul we

must always think of it as

spacious, ample and lofty; and

this can be done without the

least exaggeration, for the soul's

capacity is much greater than

we can realize.

—TERESA OF ÁVILA

Meet Teresa of Ávila

*T*magine an attractive young woman with dark, gently curling hair and a charming personality. She is Spanish, with dark eyes and an expressive manner. She is also witty, loves to talk, and wants to please others.

"Who are you?" her Beloved asked her.

"I am Teresa of Jesus," she replied. "And who are you?"

"I am Jesus of Teresa."

Or so the story goes. Teresa was a delightful combination of fierce independence, femininity, and intense spirituality. For years she struggled with a natural inclination toward frivolity and flirtation. She was described as intelligent, charming, deeply spiritual, and hardheaded. Yet, her love for the Lord won out over her natural tendencies and worldly enticements.

Teresa was born in Ávila, Spain, on March 28, 1515, to a wealthy tax collector and his second wife. Her family's mixed ancestry—part Jewish and part Christian—kept them from being accepted in the most elite levels of Spanish society despite their wealth.

Teresa, one of ten children, described herself as her father's favorite. She was extroverted and affectionate. When Teresa was only thirteen, her mother died. Her mother's death devastated her, and she poured out her grief to the Virgin Mary, praying and asking that she be her mother.

Teresa's father saw her need for wise guidance, so he sent her to a convent school in Ávila. (He was also bothered by her minor flirtations with a cousin and thought that sending her to a convent school would remedy that situation.) Surprisingly, fun-loving Teresa loved the convent life and began thinking about becoming a nun. However, about eighteen months after she entered the convent school, a serious illness forced her to return home. During her recuperation, which lasted for several years, one of her uncles introduced her to the writings of Saint Jerome, whose letters led Teresa to her decision to become a nun. Her father, voicing his disapproval, refused to give his consent.

Nevertheless, twenty-year-old Teresa's determination led her to run away to the Carmelite Convent of the Incarnation in Ávila. Her father saw that she was serious about her call to the religious life, so he resigned himself to her decision. Teresa took her final vows as a nun two years later.

Not long after taking her vows, Teresa became seriously ill again and did not respond to medical treatment. Her father brought her back home, where she steadily grew worse. She went into a coma for several days, and her legs were paralyzed for about three years. During this period of suffering, she began practicing what she called mental prayer. (Mental prayer is the same as contemplative prayer, as opposed to merely reciting liturgical prayers.)

Understandably, Teresa experienced some dry times spiritually as a result of her poor health. For a while she even stopped praying, but eventually she resumed the discipline of prayer and went back to the convent. Still she struggled with her prayer life—even though she lived a contemplative life for many years, she never felt that she had fully surrendered herself to God. Her turning point came in 1554 when, as she was praying before a statue of the wounded Christ, she experienced a profound conversion. Describing this experience, she said, "So great was my distress when I thought how ill I had repaid Him for those wounds that I felt as if my heart were breaking, and I threw myself down beside Him." Soon after this she began having intense experiences of God's presence through visions, ecstasies, and divine "locutions" (hearing God's voice).

Teresa felt God's call to reform the convents of her day, and she began the work of reform with herself by vowing to live a more perfect life. Feeling that her convent had departed from the Carmelites' original intentions, she urged her fellow nuns to live a simple, humble life uncluttered by worldly distractions. Many in her own convent did not appreciate her zeal, and Teresa's reform efforts also caused a great deal of conflict in Ávila.

In 1562 Teresa established a reformed convent for nuns who desired a more secluded spiritual life. Five years after she established her first convent, Teresa received permission to found other convents. For the rest of her life she traveled throughout Spain, establishing new convents.

Though she encountered resistance to her efforts, she was not alone. God sent her a friend and encourager in a young friar who became known as John of the Cross. Even though Teresa was twenty-seven years older than John, they became close friends and fellow reformers. Their friendship continued for nearly fifteen years.

Over the decades of her influence, Teresa wrote an autobiography (later called *The Autobiography of Saint Teresa of Jesus*) and three other books, as well as hundreds of letters. She is best known for her book *Interior Castle*, which we will examine in the first section of this book.

In *Interior Castle* Teresa envisions the soul as a castle with many rooms, which she calls mansions. The soul progresses from the first mansions to the seventh, symbolizing union with God. Teresa stresses the importance of prayer and a love relationship with "His Majesty," as she calls the Lord. While she never claims that she is writing from the depths of her own prayer experience, obviously she does so.

Despite months and even years of serious illness, Teresa persevered through her pain to the age of sixty-seven. She died in 1582 en route to visit a duchess who wanted her present when her child was born. She died as she lived: serving God and others.

Teresa's tireless efforts to reform the convents of her day made such a dramatic impact on the Catholic Church that in 1970 Pope Paul VI proclaimed her a Doctor of the Church, a title given to outstanding theological teachers and saints. She was the first woman to be honored with this title.

First Mansions

I began to think of the soul as if it were a castle made of a single diamond or of very clear crystal, in which there are many rooms, just as in Heaven there are many mansions. . . . the soul of the righteous [person] is nothing but a paradise, in which, as God tells us, [God] takes . . . delight. . . .

. . . As to what good qualities there may be in our souls, or Who dwells within them, or how precious they are—those are things which we seldom consider and so we trouble little about carefully preserving the soul's beauty. All our interest is centred in the rough setting of the diamond, and in the outer wall of the castle—that is to say, in these bodies of ours. . . .

. . . Souls without prayer are like people whose bodies or limbs are paralysed: they possess feet and hands but they cannot control them. In the same way, there are souls so infirm and so accustomed to busying themselves with outside affairs that nothing can be done for them, and it seems as though they are incapable of entering within themselves at all. So accustomed have they grown to living all the time with the reptiles and other creatures to be found in the outer court of the castle that they have almost become like them; and although by nature they are so richly endowed as to have the power of holding converse with none other than God Himself, there is nothing that can be done for them. . . .

. . . The door of entry into this castle is prayer and meditation. . . .

. . . These [who have just entered the castle] are very much absorbed in worldly affairs. . . . Full of a thousand preoccupations as they are, they pray only a few times a month, and as a rule they are thinking all the time of their preoccupations, for they are very much attached to them, and where their treasure is, there is their heart also. From time to time, however, they shake their minds free of them and it is a great thing that they should know themselves well enough to realize that they are not going the right way to reach the castle door. Eventually they enter the first rooms on the lowest floor, but so many reptiles get in with them that they are unable to appreciate the beauty of the castle or to find any peace within it. Still, they have done a good deal by entering at all.[1]

Interior Castle is easier to read than the writings of many other saints. Teresa's extended analogy of the castle with its rooms indicating spiritual progress is simple to understand. The castle symbolizes the soul. The rooms (or mansions) progress from a poorly furnished soul in the first mansions—complete with snakes—to a mature and Christlike soul in the seventh mansions. We will work through the seven mansions progressively, gleaning what help we can for our own spiritual journeys.

Teresa's analogy appeals to me greatly, since the Lord once gave me an image of myself as a large diamond. As I prayed during a retreat, a picture of a volleyball-sized diamond flashed into my mind. The huge diamond, suspended in light, shot thousands of colored prisms around me. I couldn't think what this image represented until the Lord led me to see that I was the diamond. Having never perceived myself as beautiful, I found this sunlit diamond breathtakingly beautiful. I came to understand that through the diamond image the Lord was telling me that I was beautiful in God's eyes and that I brought God much pleasure. Needless to say, I felt awed, humbled, and blessed by this prayer image. Six years later I can still see the image in my mind quite clearly.

Teresa carries the diamond image much further, claiming that the diamond is a castle that comprises our souls, the place where God dwells. She even divides it into rooms, complete with doors and walls, and mentions that reptiles are crawling outside them. Teresa compares the outer walls of the castle or the rough setting of the diamond to our bodies, which house the soul. She warns against the danger of becoming consumed with the outer setting and ignoring—and failing to preserve the beauty of—the soul.

What would she think if she lived in today's culture? Has any culture ever been as consumed with their bodies as ours? I wonder how often the average woman thinks of her soul compared with how often she thinks of her appearance. We become absorbed with our bodies at the cost of neglecting our souls.

Teresa uses the metaphor of crawling reptiles to symbolize anything that distracts us from prayer. For as long as I can remember, I have been terrified of snakes. I can't even think of them in the safety of my home without cringing. The thought of snakes crawling on the outside walls of my home is unbearable! But Teresa was not speaking of literal snakes. I think she meant to caricature our worldly interests as things that can harm us. Yet, we are so caught up in appearances—physical, professional, even spiritual—that we can't even perceive their danger to us.

She goes so far as to say that even in our prayer attempts, we let the reptiles in with us. The reptiles that intrude on our prayers rob us of any appreciation for our soul's beauty or needs, and thus we find no peace. What better description is there of our materialistic society? What change would we see in our society if women spent as much time in prayer as they spend on their appearances?

But Teresa insists that there is another enemy to prayer. We not only avoid prayer by absorption with our appearance but also by our preoccupation. Teresa claims that even when we try to pray, our worldly interests distract us. Why is this true? I believe we are overly preoccupied because we try to do too much.

If we wanted less, we might work less. In his book *Mustard Seed vs. McWorld*, Tom Sine reports that in 1973 the average American worked forty-one hours a week. By 1997 time spent at work had increased to fifty-one hours a week.[2] No wonder we have less time to pray!

Sine claims that our materialistic drive makes our lives frenetic. But perhaps we prefer to stay busy so we won't have time to meditate and pray. We think we are avoiding the reptiles; instead, we are cohabiting with them.

Teresa's picture of the souls in the first mansions is not pretty. These souls barely know they possess a soul. They live crazy lives of obsession with external preoccupations, occasionally remembering to pray but not finding peace from their reptilian pursuits even in prayer. If this picture sounds all too familiar, take heart—more mansions remain to be explored. ॐ

Reflection

1. Where do you find yourself in Teresa's analogy?

2. On what is your attention focused: your external life (preoccupied with appearances) or your internal life (the soul)? Which do you want your focus to be?

3. What are the reptiles in your lifestyle?

4. How do you make time for prayer and solitude? What is most helpful to you in these times of seeking to be in God's presence?

5. What is your real desire regarding your soul's life? What will you do to realize this desire?

Scripture

Select one or more of these readings:
- Matthew 6:19-24
- John 14:1-15
- 2 Corinthians 4:5-10
- 1 Peter 3:3-4, 15-18

Exercise

In your journal list your activities for a typical week. What physical activities and mental concerns consume your time? Pray over the list. Which items are truly necessary? Which ones could you omit in order to create more time for prayer and meditation?

Embrace the Cross

*T*his chapter has to do with those who have already begun to practise prayer and who realize the importance of not remaining in the first Mansions, but who often are not yet resolute enough to leave those Mansions, and will not avoid occasions of sin, which is a very perilous condition. But it is a very great mercy that they should contrive to escape from the snakes and other poisonous creatures [of the first Mansions] if only for short periods. . . . There is great hope that they will get farther into the castle still. . . .

. . . Nevertheless, the assault which the devils now make upon the soul, in all kinds of ways, is terrible; and the soul suffers more than in the preceding Mansions; for there it was deaf and dumb, . . . so it offered little resistance, like one who to a great extent has lost hope of gaining the victory. Here the understanding is keener and the faculties are more alert, while the clash of arms and the noise of cannon are so loud that the soul cannot help hearing them. For here the devils once more show the soul these vipers—that is, the things of the world—and they pretend that earthly pleasures are almost eternal: they remind the soul of the esteem in which it is held in the world, of its friends and relatives, of the way in which its health will be endangered by penances . . . and of impediments of a thousand other kinds. . . .

. . . Then the understanding comes forward and makes the soul realize that, for however many years it may live, it can never hope to have a better friend, for the world is full of falsehood and these pleasures which the devil pictures to it are accompanied by trials and cares and annoyances; and tells it to be certain that outside this castle it will find neither security nor peace. . . .

. . . It is a curious thing: here we are, meeting with hindrances and suffering from imperfections by the thousand, with our virtues so young that they have not yet learned how to walk . . . and yet we are not ashamed to be wanting consolations in prayer and to be complaining about periods of aridity. This must not be true of you, sisters: embrace the Cross which your Spouse bore upon His shoulders and realize that this Cross is yours to carry too.[3]

I have spent my entire life attempting to avoid pain and suffering. This excerpt about embracing the cross does not come as welcome news to me—or probably to anyone in our "comfort" culture.

I grew up in a sheltered, Christian environment in the 1950s. My, how life has changed! I didn't know much about life when I married. Information was not broadcast as freely then, whereas now I feel bombarded with information. As a teenager, I knew nothing of sex, not to mention AIDS and contraception. And, yes, ignorance was bliss.

Along with this blissful ignorance, I knew little of suffering—the world's or my own. I wasn't exposed to atrocities on the nightly news like the ones our kindergartners see now. So was my ignorance good or bad? It certainly was blissful while it lasted, but oh! The pain when the bubble burst! Innocence and ignorance kept me from many "occasions of sin," but it also bore the fruit of fear and a horror of suffering. When I realized that life wasn't as nice as I thought, I became determined to avoid suffering by any means.

Obviously, my attempts to avoid suffering haven't worked. I'd have to live in a cave to avoid knowing the gory details of suffering in our world, thanks to the news media's thorough coverage. So how do we deal with suffering in a godly way? Teresa would tell us that the answer is our attitude toward suffering. She would exhort us to embrace the cross.

Teresa says that in the second mansions, the soul is able to distinguish a bit better the ways of the world. At this point we face a test: Can we recognize the insinuations of greed, comfort, and success that infiltrate our thinking? Can we not only recognize them but even counter them with a reliance on God's word in scripture? Then we may reside in Teresa's second mansions, and we can expect to experience some suffering.

I believe that much of the struggle for Western Christians centers on the war between Christ and culture. Teresa describes this residence as a perilous position: we are not yet strong enough to avoid "occasions of sin," we experience aridity in prayer, and we are just beginning to see the value of spiritual riches over worldly promises. How often do frivolous spending, eating, and hobbies tempt us? How frequently do we complain about unsatisfying prayer times?

By residing in the second mansions, we confront the struggles of

Christian living. So what does Teresa say is the alternative? Embracing the cross.

Suffering is inevitable in this life, but our attitudes determine how we cope, she says. Teresa encourages us to face suffering in the strength of the Lord—to embrace the strength of the cross, which conquered life and death. Facing suffering in the strength of the Lord means that we look past the suffering and see the cross in its midst. Jesus experienced all the suffering we could ever encounter—emotional, mental, spiritual, and physical—and conquered it.

I have learned to face suffering head-on, to embrace it, and to go through it—clinging tightly to Jesus but facing it nonetheless. Avoiding all suffering is impossible. Fleeing it isn't an option, either. And ignoring it doesn't make the pain go away.

The only way through suffering is to embrace the cross. How do you do this? By putting one foot in front of the other, day after day, until the experience is behind you. By praying day after day for grace to do the right things for the right reasons and to keep on doing them. By meditating on the passages of Jesus' suffering and asking God for insight and help in suffering in a godly manner.

As I write, Easter is approaching, and embracing the cross of Jesus' suffering seems especially appropriate. Teresa encouraged her sisters in the convent, "Embrace the Cross which your Spouse bore upon His shoulders and realize that this Cross is yours to carry too."

Why is this cross ours to carry? Because we are to be holy, as Jesus is holy; we are to be imitators of Christ, "who for the sake of the joy that was set before him endured the cross" (Heb. 12:2). ❧

Reflection

1. What in the second mansions connects to your experience? In what way?

2. How are you trying to avoid "occasions of sin"?

3. What helps you distinguish between the things of God and the things of this world?

4. In what way have you experienced aridity in your prayer life?

5. How often do you find yourself trying to avoid suffering? What does embracing the cross mean to you?

Scripture

Read one or more of the following passages:
- Hebrews 12:1-13
- Luke 9:20-27
- John 19
- Isaiah 52:13–53:12
- Philippians 3

Exercise

Choose a painful situation in your life now and reflect on what it would mean to embrace the cross. How would it help you and/or others? How would you go about it?

Spend some time praying over this situation and write out one way in which you will "embrace the cross."

DAY THREE *Carrying Loads of Dirt*

*Y*ou will find out [we are now in the Third Mansions] if you are really detached from the things you have abandoned, for trifling incidents arise . . . which give you the opportunity to test yourselves and discover if you have obtained mastery over your passions. . . . If we have not progressed as far as this, then, as I have said, let us practise humility, which is the ointment for our wounds; if we are truly humble, God, the Physician, will come in due course, even though He tarry, to heal us.

. . . How I wish ours [love] would make us dissatisfied with this habit of always serving God at a snail's pace! As long as we do that we shall never get to the end of the road. And as we seem to be walking along and getting fatigued all the time—for, believe me, it is an exhausting road—we shall be very lucky if we escape getting lost. . . . Would it not be better to get the journey over and done with? . . .

When we proceed with all this caution, we find stumbling-blocks everywhere; for we are afraid of everything, and so dare not go farther, as if we could arrive at these Mansions by letting others make the journey for us! That is not possible, my sisters; so, for the love of the Lord, let us make a real effort: let us leave our reason and our fears in [God's] hands and let us forget the weakness of our nature which is apt to cause us so much worry. . . . Our own task is only to journey with good speed so that we may see the Lord. . . .

. . . Without complete self-renunciation, [our] state is very arduous and oppressive, because, as we go along, we are labouring under the burden of our miserable nature, which is like a great load of earth. . . . [but the Lord] always gives us much more than we deserve by granting us a spiritual sweetness much greater than we can obtain from the pleasures and distractions of this life.[4]

A major sign of spiritual maturity is losing the attitude *The one with the most toys wins*. If Teresa lived in Western culture today, she would soundly denounce our consumerism as pleasures and distractions that slow down our journey through the spiritual mansions.

American culture has become obsessed with toys. The latest toys or videos are billed as collector's items; advertisements urge us to grab them before they are gone.

Teresa reminds us to detach ourselves, to abandon these "distractions." I have several passions I frequently must rein in so I will not lose sight of the journey calling me "further in and higher up."[5] I have mentioned elsewhere my craving for beautiful things. This passion ambushes me occasionally in the form of antiques, art, or clothing. I am often tempted to spend too much on books and flowers. All of these created things themselves are good. They become worldly pleasures and distractions when they enslave me, causing me to spend money on them that should be given to kingdom purposes. They enslave me when I think I *must* have them.

Teresa says these passions slow our spiritual walk to a snail's pace. She constantly reminds us that the goal of this journey is to see the Lord. So why aren't we hurrying on, rather than strolling, toward our destination? Teresa wants us to become dissatisfied with our slow progress and hurry on to see Jesus in the upper mansions.

Teresa asks why we allow fear and other stumbling blocks to slow us, to cause us to procrastinate—as if others would make the journey for us if we just stall long enough. Teresa likens these distractions and spiritual personality flaws to carrying a heavy load of dirt.

A few years ago, my husband and I decided to build our own patio. However, we hadn't reckoned on the soil's being more clay than dirt. We shoveled out the clay dirt and hauled out wheelbarrow after wheelbarrow of this increasingly heavy stuff. Believe me, we know about heavy dirt! So this image speaks clearly to me of the load of hindrances we carry in our petty obsessions and hoarded possessions.

How do we give up our self-absorbed passion for toys? Just as we kick any other habit: We simply quit. We can stop making trips to the mall our recreation. We can make simple, healthy meals at home instead of eating out so often. We can recognize the next craze for what it is and refuse to let someone else prey upon our weaknesses and our money. Perhaps we quit watching the shopping channel or going to places that tempt us to spend indiscriminately and selfishly. If our distraction is TV, we can turn off the TV and see how much time sud-

denly appears for spiritual projects. We can confront our own spiritual apathy and call it what it is—or else we can stop bemoaning the
fact that we don't have time and money for spiritual things.

What is the reward for all this self-renunciation? The Lord will
meet us upon our arrival in the third mansions and give us "spiritual
sweetness" that is better than all the pleasures and distractions this life
can offer. The Lord offers a satisfaction so deep that material things
lose their appeal. Let us "press on toward the goal for the prize of the
heavenly call of God in Christ Jesus" (Phil. 3:14). ☙

Reflection

1. What "toys" do you cling to? Why? What can you do to let them go?

2. What personal stumbling blocks keep you from making spiritual progress?

3. On a scale of 1 to 10 (1 being lowest), how satisfied are you with your spiritual progress?

4. What is the "load of dirt" you carry? Why do you carry it?

5. What spiritual sweetness do you imagine the Lord holds out to you that would satisfy your needs?

Scripture

- Philippians 3:7-16
- Philippians 3:17-21
- Acts 4:32-37
- Acts 5:1-16
- Matthew 11:25-30

Exercise

In your journal, draw a picture to symbolize your life journey right now. You might want to draw the load you carry as well. Then look at this drawing, pray over it, and ask the Lord what to do about it.

DAY FOUR *Spiritual Sweetness*

*A*s these Mansions [we are now in the Fourth Mansions] are now getting nearer to the place where the King dwells, they are of great beauty and there are such exquisite things to be seen and appreciated in them that the understanding is incapable of describing them in any way accurately without being completely obscure to those devoid of experience. . . . It seems that, in order to reach these Mansions, one must have lived for a long time in the others; . . . but there is no infallible rule about it, as you must often have heard, for the Lord gives when He wills and as He wills and to whom He wills, and as the gifts are His own, this is doing no injustice to anyone.

Into these Mansions poisonous creatures seldom enter, and if they do, they prove quite harmless—in fact they do the soul good. I think in this state of prayer it is much better for them to enter and make war upon the soul, for, if it [the soul] had no temptations, the devil might mislead it with regard to the consolations which God gives, and do much more harm than he can when it is being tempted. The soul, too, would not gain so much, for it would be deprived of all occasions of merit and be living in a state of permanent absorption. When a soul is continuously in a condition of this kind, I do not consider it at all safe, nor do I think it possible for the Spirit of the Lord to remain in a soul continuously in this way during our life of exile. . . .

. . . We may describe as sweetness what we get from our meditations and from petitions made to Our Lord. This proceeds from our own nature, though, of course, God plays a part in the process (and in everything I say you must understand this, for we can do nothing without [God]). This spiritual sweetness arises from the actual virtuous work which we perform. . . . I have seen people shed tears over some great joy; sometimes, in fact, I have done so myself.

It seems to me that the feelings which come to us from Divine things are as purely natural as these, except that their source is nobler, although these worldly joys are in no way bad. . . .

. . . If you would progress a long way on this road and ascend to the Mansions of your desire, the important thing is not to think much, but to love much; do, then, whatever most arouses you to love. Perhaps we do not know what love is; it would not surprise me a great deal to learn this, for love consists, not in the extent of our happiness, but in the firmness of our determination to try to please God in everything, and to endeavor, in all possible ways, not to offend [God]. . . .

31

O Lord, do Thou remember how much we have to suffer on this road through lack
of knowledge! The worst of it is that, as we do not realize we need to know more when
we think about Thee, we cannot ask those who know. . . . So we suffer terrible trials
because we do not understand ourselves.[6]

Think of the most beautiful sight you have ever seen. Mentally visit that
place and relive the wonder and joy of that beauty. Now think how to
describe it so that someone else can see it as vividly as you did. Impossible?
Then think how much more difficult it must be for us to envision all that
God holds out to us in this life—not to mention heaven!

Teresa describes the fourth mansions as a place of exquisite beauty.
In part of this passage (not quoted here), she laments her inadequacy
at explaining the wonder of this spiritual sweetness available to us in
the fourth mansions. Words fail her in the same way that we struggle
to describe our beautiful place in our minds. We don't realize how
much more is available for us to enjoy when we pray and commune
with the Lord. So how could those outside the faith understand us
when we try to explain our relationship with the Lord?

I teach evening classes for adults at a Christian college. We often
begin our classes with devotions. After I shared how Christ helps me
in my daily life, I received an e-mail from a student. She said she had
never heard anyone who knew Christ personally and asked, "How do
I find God like that?"

We exchanged several e-mails and, since it was Holy Week, the next
time I saw her I loaned her my copy of *The Message* (a contemporary
paraphrase of the New Testament) and asked her to read John 14–21. I
wanted her to experience reading about Christ's Passion during the
week before Easter. She e-mailed me soon afterward, saying she had
heard this story all her life but had never understood it until now. She
thanked me profusely and said she would hurry out to find a copy of
The Message. She had already begun to taste some of that spiritual
sweetness. She said, "You will never know how much comfort I
received from reading these words."

I wanted so much to communicate to her the comfort, peace, and spiritual sweetness that Jesus can offer, but I didn't have enough words to convey it. The Holy Spirit, through the words of scripture, completed what I could not. But the story doesn't end there—how can I explain to her how much more awaits her? She is only beginning and has no idea how much more "more" can be. Similarly, no matter how far we have come, we cannot imagine how much more God would give us if we were ready to receive it.

Teresa says that to reach the fourth mansions, one must live in the others for a long time. But that doesn't seem right to me. Surely if we were willing, we could move much faster through the mansions! Why wouldn't we want to go to a place where fewer "poisonous snakes" (temptations) exist? Why would we linger in lower mansions when we could be enjoying sweeter spiritual experiences of our Lord?

How do we make faster progress spiritually? According to Teresa, spiritual progress comes not so much from thinking as from loving much. Many of us will not move on until we have it all "figured out." How often this must slow down our spiritual growth! Much of the spiritual life is not attained by understanding but by loving God enough to trust what the Word says, and then obeying it.

We cannot live a spiritual life by reason alone. The spiritual life is really about love—loving God. Augustine said: "Love, and do what thou wilt."[7] By this, he meant that if loving God is our primary goal, our actions will not be a problem. We cannot love God and sin against God or our neighbors.

Another argument against "thinking much" is that we don't know how much we don't know. Many mansions remain for us to go through and much more to understand that we can't make sense of now. We don't even know what questions to ask about the next stage (mansions), for we haven't yet journeyed that far.

We need not allow our ignorance to discourage us. Instead, we can let it serve as an incentive to forge on through the mansions of prayer and experience all that God has to offer us—in this life and the next. ❧

Reflection

1. Do you ever feel as if you have been living in the same spiritual mansion for a long time? Why do you think that is the case?

2. How often do "poisonous snakes" (temptations) visit you? How do you handle them when they come?

3. Recall an experience of spiritual sweetness. What made it sweet? Do you long for more?

4. In your spiritual journey, do you have to resist the tendency to focus on thinking more than loving?

5. What is your vision of what God offers you at this point in your life?

Scripture

Read one or more of the following passages:
- Romans 11:33-36
- Psalm 119:9-16
- Psalm 119:105-112
- Isaiah 30:20-21
- John 21:15-17

Exercise

In your journal, list your spiritual priorities for the next year—things you want to learn and actions to take. What will it take to make these genuine priorities?

Spinning Silk

*Y*ou will have heard of the wonderful way in which silk is made—a way which no one could invent but God—and how it comes from a kind of seed which looks like tiny peppercorns. . . . When the warm weather comes, and the mulberry-trees begin to show leaf, this seed starts to take life; until it has this sustenance, on which it feeds, it is as dead. The silkworms feed on the mulberry-leaves until they are full-grown. . . . They start spinning silk, making themselves very tight little cocoons, in which they bury themselves. Then, finally, the worm, which was large and ugly, comes out of the cocoon a beautiful white butterfly. . . .

. . . The silkworm is like the soul which takes life when, through the heat which comes from the Holy Spirit, it begins to utilize the help God gives to us all, and to make use of the remedies which [God] left in [the] Church—such as frequent confessions, good books, and sermons, for these are the remedies for a soul dead in negligences and sins and frequently plunged into temptation. The soul begins to live and nourishes itself on this food, and on good meditations, until it is full grown. . . .

O then, my daughters! Let us hasten to perform this task and spin this cocoon. Let us renounce our self-love and self-will, and our attachment to earthly things. Let us practise penance, prayer, mortification, obedience, and all the other good works that you know of. Let us do what we have been taught; and we have been instructed about what our duty is. Let the silkworm die—let it die, as in fact it does when it has completed the work which it was created to do. Then we shall see God and shall ourselves be as completely hidden in [God's] greatness as is this little worm in its cocoon. . . .

. . . When it is in this state of prayer, and quite dead to the world, [the worm] comes out a little white butterfly.[8]

Lately the evils of this world have been weighing on me. School shootings, abortions, oppression around the world, poverty, and my own pain nearly cause me—an optimist—to despair. Where is God's sovereign hand in all this? Where are justice and righteousness? I often have to remind myself that God's work quietly and often invisibly continues despite the evils of this world.

Teresa reminds me of that with her image of the silkworm. Worms are not attractive nor thought valuable (unless you're going fishing). But silkworms are fascinating! The humble-looking worm on the mulberry leaves is spinning quietly but accomplishing something at the same time.

A worm, cloaked in silk, is surely an example of God's humorous irony—and another lesson in God's subversive ways of accomplishing the beautiful.

Our God is the God of little things, humble things, quietly and often invisibly accomplishing divine purposes. No one hears worms chewing or notices a cocoon quietly forming. And who could guess that something as humble appearing as a cocoon contains our most valuable and beautiful fabric? Teresa noticed and calls us to pay attention to the beauty of the inner and quiet workings of God.

Teresa compares the soul (in the fifth mansions) to a silkworm. Just as the silkworm eats mulberry leaves, she says, so we need to take in spiritual sustenance by means of confession, good books, and sermons—an interesting trio.

My husband and I spent Easter weekend this year at Saint Meinrad Archabbey in southern Indiana. What bliss it was to spend three full days thinking about the Passion and Resurrection of Christ. I learned many things from the humble Benedictine monks there. One of their preparatory practices for Easter entails a time of confession and reconciliation. I was reminded of how rarely we hear of confession in Christian practice. To confess my sins before my fellow Christians and ask forgiveness would surely bear fruit for heavenly use. Why, then, don't we confess more often? Do pride and fear prevent us from doing that? Confession, and its resulting purity, would have far-reaching benefits.

As for Teresa's admonition to read good books, I can personally testify to the benefits of this practice. Good books are one of the joys of my life. I usually read three or four books simultaneously. Most mornings I read a chapter of some spiritual book during my time with God. I am usually reading a book to prepare for teaching a class. In addition, I often read a psychological/spiritual book, and I read classical literature at night before going to sleep. Many other types of books—art, history, poetry—fill in the odd cracks of my time. Teresa says we should read *good* books—which means we need to carefully choose reading material that will edify the soul and not just serve as escapism.

Sermons are a more subjective matter than confession and books. Finding solid, biblical preaching to feed our souls is no easy task. The preaching I've most appreciated comes from those who hear God speak through the Bible. Sometimes being open to hear God speaking is difficult. In the sixteenth century Teresa probably heard very different sermons from the ones we hear today, but the Word has not changed. It still feeds our souls the food we most need.

Teresa also mentions prayer, self-renunciation, obedience, and all good works—which all five women in this book recommend as standard equipment. Spiritual disciplines are the Christian's sustenance. Although we may dislike the regimen, we cannot deny the rich results. Teresa compares disciplines to the silkworm eating seeds. Somehow the seeds are transformed into spiritual food that enables spiritual maturity. Even though we can't see the process happening, it is still real. I am coming to believe that life's greatest realities are the invisible ones.

My lingering impression from our weekend at Saint Meinrad's was the immensity of the invisible work the monks do—quietly transforming the world by their prayers. They live tucked away in a quiet, remote valley. They stay up all night praying the Psalms and keeping vigil for Easter until dawn. Their continual prayer and devotion to worship quietly changes the world. God's subversive work is evidenced in the overthrow of evil and social injustice.

Prayer unobtrusively holds the universe together and creates beauty within a world of sin. The only way we'll ever soar is to first renounce the ways of the world and then feed on the subversive and spiritual seeds of God. ❧

Reflection

1. What of this silkworm imagery appeals to you?

2. In what stage of spiritual development do you see yourself right now—worm, cocoon, or butterfly? Why?

3. What spiritual discipline is feeding your soul just now?

4. In what area do you feel a need for honest confession? Can you think of someone you trust to hear your confession?

5. When you reach the butterfly stage, what changes do you believe will be evident in your daily life?

Scripture

Choose one or more of the following passages to read and meditate upon:
- Matthew 13:31-36, 44
- Romans 1:18-27
- Psalm 8
- Joshua 7:1-26
- Ezekiel 3:1-11

Exercise

Write a prayer of confession in your journal. Pray that God will direct you to someone you can trust to be your confessor. Ask that person to hear your confession of sins and to pray for you.

Hair Shirts

Thou woundest not, yet pain'st indeed,
And painlessly the soul is freed
From love of creatures. . . .[9]

*Y*ou are doing very well, glory be to God, as regards the kind of meditation you are making—I mean when you are not experiencing a state of quiet. . . .

I send you this hair-shirt to use when you find it difficult to recollect yourself at times of prayer, or when you are anxious to do something for the Lord. It is good for awakening love, but you are on no account to put it on after you are dressed, or to sleep in it. . . . Even a mere nothing like this makes one so happy when it is done for God, out of a love for [God] like the love you are feeling now, that I don't want us to omit giving it a trial. . . . Write and tell me how you get on with this trifle. For I assure you, the more faithfully we deal with ourselves, remembering Our Lord's sufferings, the more of a trifle it seems to us. It makes me laugh to think how you send me sweets and presents and money, and I send you hair-shirts.[10]

You must use the discipline only for short periods, too, for in that way you feel it all the more, and at the same time it will do you less harm. Do not punish yourself with it too severely, for it is of no great importance, though you will think it very imperfect of you not to. . . .

. . . And remember, if it affects the kidneys, you must neither wear the hair-shirt nor take the discipline, or it will do you great harm. God prefers your health, and your obedience, to your penances.[11]

My confessor, Dr. Velazquez, was here to-day. I discussed with him what you said about wanting to give up using the carpets and silver. . . . In this, however, he agreed with me. He says it is of no importance one way or the other; what matters is that you should try to see how unimportant such things are and not become attached to them. . . . So just be patient for now: God always gives us opportunities to carry out our good desires, and [God] will give you a chance to carry out yours. May God watch over you for me and make you very holy. Amen.[12]

When God takes possession of the soul, He gives it more and more dominion over created things, and even if [God's] presence is withdrawn and the satisfaction which the soul was enjoying disappears, . . . [God] does not withdraw Himself from the soul, nor does it fail to grow very rich in graces, and, as time goes on, that becomes evident in the affections.[13]

Imagine discipling a brother or sister in the ways of God and prayer. Teresa was evidently doing just that through her letters. Her brother's desire to please God was causing him to question:

- How can I pray without being so distracted?
- What else can I do to please God?
- Do I need to give up my earthly treasures (carpet and silver) to live a life that pleases God?

We ask all of these questions at critical points in our spiritual development. Teresa's answers contain a few surprises, certainly to our modern, comfort-minded approach to spiritual growth.

I believe the motto for spiritual growth in our day is "What's the easiest path to sainthood?" or "How can I become a saint in two weeks?" These sound like those miraculous diets touted on the front of women's magazines. Aren't ease and comfort the bottom line in our culture? I'm no less susceptible than anyone else. I would love to be able to lose ten pounds effortlessly or to become a saint in one easy prayer time.

What action does Teresa recommend? Wearing hair shirts. That seems rather drastic to us today. People wore hair shirts in an attempt to suffer for God and thus be drawn closer to the Almighty. Many monks also practiced self-flagellation—beating themselves with leather thongs—for the same purpose. Some saints went without food or stood outside in freezing weather to deny their fleshly desires for comfort and physical pleasures, which they saw as enemies of spiritual growth.

Comfort held no place in the ancient concept of spiritual progress. We can rationalize and say that life was already harder for them, and they didn't mind discomfort as much as we do. Who *wouldn't* mind standing outside in freezing temperatures? We can't help but admire their attempts to please God.

Since God does not require us to wear hair shirts or starve ourselves, what else can we do to please God? Simply, whatever God asks of us. My experience is that whatever God asks me to renounce may seem absurd to you. Let's say you are a smoker, and God asks you to give up cigarettes. To me, that would be no sacrifice at all. I don't smoke, so giving up cigarettes would require no sacrifice of comfort at all. But if God were to ask me to give up reading fiction or eating cookies—ah, now that would be sacrifice.

God knows that our overattachments—those habits or things that get more attention than the Almighty—need to go! Wearing a hair shirt wouldn't be comfortable, but it wouldn't necessarily help me spiritually either. Frankly, I can't see how wearing such a garment would help a person concentrate on prayer. But I suspect that the fact that some were willing to do that must have pleased God.

As to whether her brother needed to give up his carpet and silver, Teresa's advice seems sound to me. Penance is unimportant unless you become overly attached to things, she says.

I remember how a Scottish friend, Rosiland, illustrated this concept for me. Rosiland had a lovely pottery bowl with the skyline of the ancient city of Saint Andrews crafted along its rim. I had admired it, and the next time I visited her, she gave me the bowl. When I protested, she said: "I do like it—too much. I want to give it to you so it doesn't have too great a hold on my affections." I have never forgotten that practical, spiritual discipline of simplicity and keeping God first in her affections. As Teresa would say, "Painlessly the soul is freed from love of creatures" [created things].

Teresa's brother was well on his way to maturity in Christ in his desire to

• pray well,

• please God with his life,

• give up whatever comfort stood in the way of the second goal. These three principles would help all of us, if we would spend time translating them into action. ✍

Reflection

1. Which of these three principles is hardest for you to live faithfully? Why?

2. How do you define your comfort zone? What comfort would be hardest for you to give up (to enable spiritual growth)?

3. What "hair shirt" could or should you employ in your life?

4. What thoughts or situations most often distract you from praying as you'd like?

5. What changes could you make in order to live a life that is more pleasing to God?

Scripture

Read one or more of the following:
- 1 Corinthians 9:24-27
- 2 Timothy 2
- 2 Corinthians 1:3-11
- Psalm 20

Exercise

In your journal, list all your "must have" comforts. Meditate on why these things or habits are so important to you. Then ask yourself: What on this list is not pleasing to God? What is purely selfish and benefits no one but me?

Pray over this list for several days and discern whether you have listed anything that displeases the Lord.

Souls Like Beehives

*I*n speaking of the soul we must always think of it as spacious, ample and lofty; and this can be done without the least exaggeration, for the soul's capacity is much greater than we can realize. . . . It is very important that no soul which practises prayer, whether little or much, should be subjected to undue constraint or limitation. Since God has given it such dignity, it must be allowed to roam through these mansions. . . . It must not be compelled to remain for a long time in one single room—not, at least, unless it is in the room of self-knowledge. . . . However high a state a soul may have attained, self-knowledge is [critical] and this it [the soul] will never be able to neglect, even should it so desire. Humility must always be doing its work [in the soul] like a bee making its honey in the hive: without humility, all will be lost. Still, we should remember that the bee is constantly flying about from flower to flower, and in the same way, . . . the soul must sometimes emerge from self-knowledge and soar aloft in the meditation upon the greatness and the majesty of its God. Doing this will help [the soul] to realize its own baseness better than thinking of its own nature, and it will be freer from the reptiles which enter the first rooms—that is, the rooms of self-knowledge. For although, as I say, it is through the abundant mercy of God that the soul studies to know itself, yet one can have too much of a good thing, . . . and believe me, we shall reach much greater heights of virtue by thinking upon the virtue of God than if we stay in our own little plot of ground and tie ourselves down to it completely.[14]

A couple of years ago, I taught a psychology class on *imago dei* (the image of God, in which humans were created). Before that time I had rather general thoughts about this concept, but preparing for this class forced me to define what I believe comprises God's image in us.

I generally tend to think holistically—that we are an integrated whole: mind, body, soul, and spirit. The Old Testament world had no concept of dividing human life into parts. Humans were a seamless whole with varied functions of mind, body, and spirit. People of this time did not categorize things as sacred and secular—to them, all of life belonged to God and was therefore good. They considered all human activity to be some form of worship, and that eliminated any conflict between sacred and secular. In the Old Testament realm of thought, defining *imago dei* was much easier; humanity personified God in some visible way.

The Hebrew and Greek words for *soul* intertwine with our modern perceptions of *heart* and *mind*. The soul is somehow the essence of who we are—what is most "me." The soul also determines and defines my relationship with God. The soul perceives God and responds to God. In some way, my soul personifies a part of God's creation, or even God's being. The Old Testament view would go a step further and say that my soul, which defines who I really am, also determines my actions.

Thus, if my soul is in right relationship with God, I act godly—I am godly. If my soul is corrupt, then my whole life is manifestly corrupt.

Obviously, Teresa lived under a different philosophy in the sixteenth century—a philosophy that separated and elevated the soul above other facets of human life. Her work *Interior Castle* focuses primarily on the soul's travels through mansions, or levels of development toward godliness. So she goes to great lengths to describe the soul. And, while I prefer to think holistically, it won't hurt us to focus more attention on our souls.

Teresa describes the soul as spacious, ample, and lofty. I remember once having a sensation in prayer that I was entering a vastly spacious area, opening out in front of me. I wonder if that image depicted my soul? Teresa would say so, I think.

She goes on to suggest that we avoid restricting the soul if at all possible. I wonder what Teresa would say to the infinite number of soul-cramping possibilities in our culture. We live with such an onslaught of information and noise that the soul is hardly ever free just to *be*, let alone expand.

Space, nature, and silence are prerequisites for a healthy soul. Solitude in nature, in my opinion, is great for the soul. The sheer, cathartic relief that can be found in a walk alone in a lovely spot is worth sacrificing other activities. We could relieve much of this life's anxiety by regularly setting aside time to be alone with nature.

According to Teresa, the goal of empty time and space for the soul is to increase our self-knowledge. Most of us define ourselves by what we do or by those persons to whom we are related. But we are so much more than that. We are souls that are precious to God—we bear the image of God. And our souls crave space to stretch and pray and encompass even more of God. Teresa invites us—perhaps even commands us—to explore different rooms of ourselves, much like bees know every room in the honeycomb.

We do not have to live cramped lives full of "reptiles," ignorant of ourselves or of God. God gives us spacious souls with the potential to soar as we meditate and unite our souls with God's heart. As we become closer to God, not only do we feel our own inadequacy, but we also become aware of God's abundant mercy—which more than compensates for any of our shortcomings.

Let's make it our goal to explore our spacious souls room by room, discovering who we are in God and the persons we can become by God's grace. ❧

Reflection

1. How have you envisioned your soul: spacious or cramped? Why?

2. What life situations cramp your soul?

3. When did you last schedule time to spend a morning or afternoon with God?

4. What will you have to empty from your schedule to gain self-knowledge and more knowledge of God?

5. What scares you about gaining self-knowledge?

Scripture

Read one or more of the following passages:
- Psalm 42
- Matthew 10:28-42
- Psalm 63
- Psalm 131
- Mark 8:34-38

Exercise

Meditate a while about your soul. Draw a picture to represent the rooms of your soul. Which rooms have you explored? Which ones remain un-explored? To which room might God be inviting you now?

Spend time praying over the health of your soul.

We Are God's Garden, Part 1 ❧

*T*he beginner must think of [herself] as of one setting out to make a garden in which the Lord is to take . . . delight, yet in soil most unfruitful and full of weeds. His Majesty uproots the weeds and will set good plants in their stead [place]. Let us suppose that this is already done—that a soul has resolved to practise prayer and has already begun to do so. We have now, by God's help, like good gardeners, to make these plants grow, and to water them carefully, so that they may not perish, but may produce flowers which shall send forth great fragrance to give refreshment to this Lord of ours, so that [the Lord] may often come into the garden to take . . . pleasure and have . . . delight among these virtues.

Let us now consider how this garden can be watered, so that we may know what we have to do, what labour it will cost us, if the gain will outweigh the labour, and for how long this labour must be borne. It seems to me that the garden can be watered in four ways: by taking the water from a well, which costs us great labour; or by a water-wheel and buckets, when the water is drawn by a windlass . . . or by a stream or a brook, which waters the ground much better, for it saturates it more thoroughly and there is less need to water it often, so that the gardener's labour is much less; or by heavy rain, when the Lord waters it with no labour of ours, a way incomparably better than any of those which have been described. . . .

Beginners in prayer . . . are those who draw up the water out of the well: . . . a very laborious proceeding, for it will fatigue them to keep their senses recollected, which is a great labour because they have been accustomed to a life of distraction. . . . They have to endeavour to meditate upon the life of Christ, and this fatigues their minds. Thus far we can make progress by ourselves—of course with the help of God, for without that, . . . we cannot think a single good thought. This is what is meant by beginning to draw up water from the well.[15]

When my family lived in Australia, I learned about real gardening. In Melbourne, the soil was volcanic and rich. Anything would grow in it. I learned to propagate plants just by breaking off a geranium stalk, sticking it in the ground, and *voilà*—a new geranium! We lived in two houses without gardens, and I developed luxuriant gardens in both places mostly by propagation—and a lot of sweat, but how I enjoyed it.

Gardening became one of my great passions. In such a temperate climate, roses would bloom all winter if you didn't prune them back. Pruning the roses always required great courage and discipline, because I had to deprive myself of their beauty for a while. But I knew that pruning would result in healthier roses in the spring.

So Teresa's gardening metaphor provides me with a natural metaphor for understanding prayer. Yes, even in Australia I had to deal with weeds. You can't do anything with weeds except pull them up and discard them. How like the distractions and meaningless "attachments" the Lord must weed out of us. If the Lord did not do so, we'd most likely fill our "flower beds" (souls) with weeds rather than virtues. According to Teresa, virtues are the goal of our prayer gardens. We do not grow such a garden to show off our own accomplishments.

We receive benefits in exchange for the pain we experience when the Lord pulls up our weeds; in return, God replaces our weeds with good plants. When we give up the weeds of wasted time, wasted energy, or wasted money, God generously rewards us with higher interests in kingdom values. We will find much greater meaning and satisfaction in devoting ourselves to meeting the needs of oppressed women and children, combating poverty, and working for justice than in going on a spending spree at the mall.

The virtues of compassion, generous giving, and intercessory prayer not only meet the needs of others but also nourish our own deep needs. We find ourselves more fulfilled than we ever dreamed, compared with the ephemeral and shabby recreation our materialistic culture offers.

So how does Teresa suggest we water our gardens? By spending time in prayer. She directs the gardening analogy toward the one "resolved to practise prayer." She outlines four methods of watering the flowers [virtues]. In our next session, we will look at the other three. Today's session relates to beginners in prayer.

Beginners in prayer "draw up the water" by the bucketful. I have never used a bucket to draw water from a well, so I can only imagine how much effort that requires. But I do know that carrying a five-gallon bucket to water those far reaches of my garden fatigued my arms almost immediately.

The physical effort is Teresa's analogy for how much effort it takes for beginners in prayer to stay centered (concentrated on prayer and free of distractions). I know a lot about this. Keeping my mind on God when a thousand other thoughts vie for my attention is hard work indeed—probably as challenging mentally as the physical challenge of carrying buckets of water.

The idea of meditation is foreign and unappealing to many people. Keeping your mind blank and focused on God sounds impossible and unproductive. Beginners may be tempted to give up—but don't! Sitting quietly in the presence of the Lord brings its own reward. The Lord enjoys just being with us. We discover that we needn't always be performing to please God. The goal of meditation is just being together with God.

Reading Henri Nouwen's account in *Gracias!* of his attempts to sit and meditate without distractions helped me immensely. He said he never felt satisfied with his efforts and often felt nothing at all. But a desire for that "wasted" time with God made him continue trying, and over time, he knew he was being transformed at some deep place that he had not even known in himself. Teresa invites us to experience this kind of transformation.

I too have struggled to focus on God and hold distractions at bay. Two methods help me stay centered:

1. I place my hands over my eyes to block out all light (and the world).
2. I imagine a river swiftly flowing at my feet, mentally place my distractions on the river, and watch them float downstream. Then I try to focus on the Lord and keep the river empty of distractions.

I have learned to use scripture as a focus for my meditation. I read the passage slowly and meditatively several times, trying to mine it for deeper meaning. I sit with a word or a phrase that catches my attention. Then I focus my meditation on that word or phrase and trust that the Lord is speaking to me through it. The Psalms and Isaiah have proved fruitful scriptures for my meditation.

Good books on prayer and meditation abound, but reading books cannot replace actually practicing meditation. We must haul up the water, or the prayer experience needed, to grow our own flowers so that we can delight the Lord. ✒

Reflection

1. What kind of soil is your prayer garden? How full of weeds is it? What are these weeds?

2. Have you resolved to practice prayer? How did you come to that resolution?

3. Does prayer ever seem more like a duty than a desire? How fatiguing is prayer for you?

4. What grows in your virtue garden that delights the Lord?

5. Have you ever practiced meditation? What was your experience like? What keeps you from making a habit of meditation and prayer?

Scripture

Read one or more of the following passages:

- Psalm 119:25-32
- Psalm 103
- Philippians 4:8-9
- 2 Corinthians 10:3-5
- Isaiah 55:8-13

Exercise

On a large piece of paper, draw a picture of your prayer garden. Depict the virtues as well as the weeds. What is beautiful and praiseworthy? What weeds are choking out the flowers?

Picture the Lord enjoying time to sit and gaze at your life.

We Are God's Garden, Part 2

*B*y using a device of windlass and buckets, the gardener draws more water with less labour and is able to take some rest instead of being continually at work. It is this [second] method, applied to the prayer called the Prayer of Quiet, that I now wish to describe.

This state, in which the soul begins to recollect itself, borders on the supernatural, to which it could in no way attain by its own exertions. . . . This state is a recollecting of the faculties within the soul, so that its fruition of that contentment may be of greater delight. But the faculties are not lost, nor do they sleep. The will alone is occupied, in such a way that, without knowing how, it becomes captive. It allows itself to be imprisoned by God, as one who well knows itself to be the captive of [the One] Whom it loves. . . .

Everything that now takes place brings the greatest consolation, and so little labour is involved that, even if prayer continues for a long time, it never becomes wearisome.[16]

Let us now go on to speak of the third water with which this garden is watered—that is, of running water proceeding from a river or a spring. This irrigates the garden with much less trouble. . . . But the Lord is now pleased to help the gardener, so that [God] may almost be said to be the gardener Himself, for it is [the Lord] Who does everything. . . . The pleasure and sweetness and delight are incomparably greater than in the previous state, for the water of grace rises to the very neck of the soul. . . . This seems to me to be nothing less than an all but complete death to everything in the world and a fruition of God. I know no other terms in which to describe it or to explain it, nor does the soul, at such a time, know what to do; it knows not whether to speak or to be silent, whether to laugh or to weep. This state is a glorious folly, a heavenly madness, in which true wisdom is acquired, and a mode of fruition in which the soul finds the greatest delight.[17]

In this state of prayer to which we have now come [the fourth method of watering], there is no feeling, but only rejoicing, unaccompanied by any understanding of the thing in which the soul is rejoicing. . . . In this rejoicing all the senses are occupied, so that none of them is free or able to act in any way, either outwardly or inwardly. . . . Speaking now of this rain which comes from Heaven to fill and saturate the whole of this garden with an abundance of water, we can see how much rest the gardener would be able to have if the Lord never ceased to send it whenever it was necessary. . . .

While seeking God in this way, the soul becomes conscious that it is fainting almost completely away, in a kind of swoon, with an exceeding great and sweet delight.[18]

To condense the next three stages into one meditation is a ridiculous goal. Teresa writes many long pages on each stage of watering the garden, her analogy for growth in prayer. She fills much of this space with ecstatic praise. Her long sentences have so many phrases that she occasionally loses her train of thought and has to say "and now back to my point . . ." But the effort to pinpoint her meaning is well repaid, for she paints a picture of prayer as we have never dreamed it!

Teresa equates the second method—using a bucket and windlass (or crank)—with the soul's being centered for the Prayer of Quiet. The Prayer of Quiet implies more than simple silence. For Teresa, it involves a stillness and silence that few of us ever sit long enough to achieve. It involves meditating long enough to conquer our distractions and paying sole and serious attention to God.

Spending long periods of time in prayer was common for these saintly women—but this may sound strange or even forbidding to us. However, Teresa paints the Prayer of Quiet as one that provides great consolation. She even spells out for us that long periods of prayer will not feel wearisome. Why doesn't everyone strive to reach this state of prayer? Because, Teresa says, it involves taking the will captive.

Our more common word for "the will" is *discipline*. We simply do not discipline ourselves to sit meditatively for long periods of prayer. But we must move beyond the idea that prayer is a chore. For Teresa, and all of those who reach this state of prayer, it is a joy—but that happy result is reached only by disciplining the will and the mind to sit still and focus on God alone. We first crank up the bucket of water (discipline ourselves to sit still), and the water becomes its own reward.

The third method of watering the garden is with a river or spring, or natural irrigation. In this state of prayer, the gardener has little to do, thanks to the Lord's help. Teresa commends this state as one of "pleasure and sweetness and delight . . . incomparably greater than in the previous state." She tells us that the water of grace rises up to the neck of the soul. Both pictures stress abundance of water, abundance of the Lord's help and grace. No wonder the pleasure is so great. Teresa heaps superlatives: "glorious folly," "heavenly madness," "true wisdom," "fruition," and "greatest delight." Why don't we drop everything and seek this "greatest delight"? I wonder how many of us believe we could ever attain this state of prayer. At this point, Teresa begins to sound a bit far gone with heavenly madness herself. Is this type of glorious prayer only for saints and fools, or is it available to you and me?

I believe Teresa speaks to all of us. She was writing this, her autobiography, to all her sisters in the convent. Surely all of them weren't 99 percent saint yet. And isn't this our deep longing—to know God at some ecstatic level that would transcend our earthly round of laundry and to-do lists?

I confess to a desire for escape—escape from evil and earthly limitations. It wouldn't take much to entice me to walk away from all I know in this life and escape into some heavenly realm of prayer. But the saints never advise prayer as an escape from life. No, prayer is meant to ground us and to be used for the good of others, not just our own pleasure. And can this third state be transcended? Yes, Teresa offers yet another stage of prayer.

The fourth stage is entirely of the Lord—the Lord of all gardens supplies rain abundantly and as needed—and is the object of all of our prayers. In this ultimate state of prayer, Teresa says that union with God is complete. The gardener does not have to exert any effort but simply rejoices in the rain. In fact, the gardener literally is fainting with the sweet delight of the fruit-producing rain sent by the heavenly Gardener. This state of prayer is the fruit of all the earlier efforts in disciplining the will, sitting quietly, and meditating regularly.

Gardening is an appropriate analogy for prayer. In the early stages the gardener puts in most of the effort. But after the gardener cultivates the ground, plants, and waters, the rest is up to the Lord of the harvest. The same is true of prayer. We must put forth the effort that only we can make and then wait for God to bless us (rain on us) with divine presence. Spending time in God's presence is the goal of prayer and its own reward at the same time. We can find everything we've ever desired in the presence of the Lord.

Teresa summarizes her sentiments by saying, "Oh, my Jesus and Lord, how much Thy love now means to us! It binds our own love so straitly [tightly] that at that moment it leaves us no freedom to love anything but Thee."[19]

Reflection

1. With which of these do you identify? Why?

2. Are you able to discipline your will to sit still for a Prayer of Quiet? Why or why not?

3. How do you feel about long periods of prayer? Are they appealing or unappealing? Why do you think this is so?

4. Does the idea of emotional experiences in prayer frighten you?

5. What percentage of your prayer life is your effort, and what percentage is God's? How much space do you give God to respond?

Scripture

Select one or more of the following passages for meditation:
- Psalm 55
- Luke 6:12
- Philippians 4:6-7
- Psalm 23:1-3
- Psalm 130

Exercise

If possible, find a flower garden where you can sit and reflect undisturbed. Spend ten to fifteen minutes observing the flowers, the soil, the weeds (if any).

Then compare your inner (virtue) garden to the effortless growth of the flowers before you. Ask God to help you enjoy prayer and God's cultivation of your soul.

Awakening the Soul

*T*he Lord also is in the habit of sending the most grievous infirmities. This is a much greater trial, especially if the pains are severe . . . For they affect the soul both outwardly and inwardly, till it becomes so much oppressed as not to know what to do with itself, and would much rather suffer any martyrdom than these pains. Still at the very worst, they do not last so long. . . . For, after all, God gives us no more than we can bear, and He gives us patience first. . . .

I am straining every nerve, sisters, to explain to you this operation of love, yet I do not know of any way of doing so. . . .

. . . I have just been wondering if my God could be described as the fire in a lighted brazier, from which some spark will fly out and touch the soul, in such a way that it will be able to feel the burning heat of the fire; but, as the fire is not . . . hot enough to burn it up, and the experience is very delectable, the soul continues to feel that pain and the mere touch suffices to produce that effect in it. . . . this delectable pain, which is really not pain, is not continuous: sometimes it lasts for a long time, while sometimes it suddenly comes to an end, according to the way in which the Lord is pleased to bestow it, for it is a thing which no human means can procure. Our Lord . . . has other methods of awakening the soul. Quite unexpectedly, when engaged in vocal prayer and not thinking of interior things, it [the soul] seems, in some wonderful way, to catch fire. It is just as though there suddenly assailed it a fragrance so powerful that it diffused itself through all the senses . . . to convey a consciousness that the Spouse is there. The soul is moved by a delectable desire to enjoy [God], and this disposes it to make many acts and to sing praises to Our Lord. This is what is most usually felt by the soul [in the sixth mansions]. . . .

There is another way in which God awakens the soul, . . . by means of locutions . . . Some of them seem to come from without; others from the innermost depths of the soul; others from its higher part; while others, again, are so completely outside the soul that they can be heard with the ears, and seem to be uttered by a human voice. . . . A single word of this kind—just a "Be not troubled"—is sufficient to calm [the soul]. No other word need be spoken; a great light comes to [the soul]; and all its trouble is lifted from it. . . .

One [other] kind of rapture is this. The soul, though not actually engaged in prayer, is struck by some word, which it either remembers or hears spoken by God. His Majesty is moved with compassion at having seen the soul suffering so long through its yearning for [God], and seems to be causing the spark of which we have already spoken to grow within it, so that, like the phoenix, it catches fire and springs into new life. . . .

When the soul is in this state of suspension and the Lord sees fit to reveal to it certain mysteries, such as heavenly things and imaginary visions, it is able subsequently to describe these [visions], for they are so deeply impressed upon the memory that they can never again be forgotten. . . . at [other] times come visions of so sublime a kind that it is not fitting for those who live on earth to understand them in such a way that they can describe them.[20]

Once Teresa reaches the fifth, sixth, and seventh mansions, she struggles to explain her visions in terms we "mere humans" can understand. In describing the sixth mansions, she refers to four manifestations of the spiritual in physical and sensual terms. (By *sensual*, I refer to use of the five senses, not a sexually limited definition.) Invisibility and lack of tangibility frustrate and frighten us. We want a God "with skin"— one that we can see and feel. Teresa takes eleven chapters to describe the sensual experiences of God that take place in the sixth mansions.

The first way Teresa mentions of awakening the soul is through *suffering*. She describes her own physical suffering, although she cloaks her identity in "I know a person who . . ." Not long after taking her final vows as a nun, Teresa fell gravely ill. For four days she was in a coma, and everyone despaired of her recovery. When she awoke, she was so weak that she had to be carried around in a sheet for eight months. Then she began to recover, but it took two more years before she could even crawl on hands and knees. Eventually she was able to walk again, but her digestive system was ruined, and she lived in constant pain for the rest of her days.

Teresa knew both God and physical suffering, and she didn't hesitate to claim that God had sent the suffering. Yet she never expected life with God to mean life without suffering.

I must confess to cringing when I read her statement, "The Lord is also in the habit of sending the most grievous infirmities." With the advantages of technology, years of research, and modern medicine, many people tend to expect healing of almost any condition. As believers, we often assume that God's will is healing. But God intends healing of *souls*, which are eternal. And the Great Physician uses the extremities of our lives to bring about that soul healing.

In my own life, the most difficult situations have also proved to be the most productive times for spiritual growth—because I was most desperate for God's help. I have learned to trust that God is working, whether or not I can tangibly verify it.

The second method God uses to awaken souls, according to Teresa, is *a sudden "consciousness that the Spouse [God] is there."* During prayer, she says, the soul seems to suddenly "catch fire," or become suddenly aware of God's presence. Teresa compares this igniting of the soul with being struck by a powerful fragrance.

God still intervenes in our dailyness and provides us a moment of intimacy with the divine. Sometimes this happens as we are praying or reading God's Word, but sometimes it occurs during an ordinary activity. I remember one such experience. I had stopped at a red light in Melbourne, Australia, waiting for a commuter train to pass. I stared at the windshield wipers and suddenly became vitally aware of God's presence in the car with me. For a brief but heavenly moment, I didn't hear the train or see the wipers but was transfixed by the nearness of God. I was overjoyed by the Lord's intervention in my daily routine. I still think of this incident as a precious reminder of how God's ever-present love surrounds our earthly activities. Teresa is correct—awareness of God's presence does awaken the soul.

The third way Teresa says that God awakens souls is through the use of *locutions*. Evidently she refers to some phenomenon—some individual way that God speaks to the soul. One source defines *locutions* like this:

> Locutions of supernatural origin cannot be produced at will; they are distinct, causing fervor, peace, humility, and obedience. Intellectual locutions are words or statements perceived immediately by the intellect without the aid of the external sense or imagination. . . .
>
> Successive intellectual locutions are a kind of dialogue or conversation between the Holy Spirit and the soul.[21]

Does Teresa mean that she actually heard words from God? Probably so, but whether the message was audible is irrelevant. Somehow God imprinted a message upon her soul. For Teresa and most women saints, intimate communication was central to their relationship with God. They often referred to God as their heavenly Spouse. Experiences of hearing God's words or seeing visions was not unusual for the saints.

How might we receive words, or messages, from God today? Perhaps certain words grab our attention as we read scripture. The words "catch fire," as Teresa suggested; they seem written especially for us. Sometimes another person is the vehicle for God's message to us, and we know deep within that the person's words are truly from God. At other times, we will sense messages or verses that seem to drop into our minds. In a recent prayer session for discernment, I heard: "This is the way; walk in it." I recognized the Lord's voice in these words, a quotation from Isaiah 30:21. When God wants to communicate with us, no limitations exist on creative ways to do so.

The fourth method of awakening souls, Teresa says, is through *visions*. Visions may occur less often these days because our frantic culture spends so little time listening and meditating on God. Peter's vision occurred while he was praying (Acts 10). Sometimes visions come in dreams, at other times in a state somewhere between waking and sleeping. However a vision comes, God knows how to convince us where the vision came from. God also knows exactly when a vision is needed and who needs it.

One of my students, Jim, recently told me how God called him to ministry through a vision. Jim was hunting and suddenly had a vision of Christ present there in the woods. All the animals bowed down before Christ, who then took Jim's hand and led him out of the woods. Jim interpreted this vision as a call to stop hunting and enter the ministry.

In summary, Teresa says that suffering, a special awareness of God's presence, locutions, and visions are God's sensual means of awakening the soul. We humans can't even perceive our own spiritual deadness and blindness. However, we need not worry, for the Lord will do for us exactly what we most need to awaken and unite our souls with our heavenly "Spouse." ❧

Reflection

1. What is your response to the thought of suffering as a means of spiritual awakening?

2. When have you had a verse or a moment "catch fire" with the presence of God? What was that like?

3. What was your most meaningful experience of hearing words from God especially spoken to you?

4. In what ways does the idea of a vision scare you? Why might God use a vision or a dream to communicate with you?

5. From what slumber does your soul need awakening?

Scripture

Meditate on one or more of the following passages:
- Acts 10:9-23
- Luke 1:10-25
- Luke 1:26-38

Exercise

For a week, try practicing a more sensitive awareness of God in all your surroundings. Listen to nature, watch it, and look for God's presence. Look for the image of God in each person you meet. Spend extra time listening in prayer and meditating on the Word after reading it. Make a habit of trying to find God with your senses.

The Lord's chief desire is to

reveal Himself to you and, in

order for Him to do that, He

gives you abundant grace.

—MADAME JEANNE GUYON

Meet Madame Guyon

Jeanne Guyon (1648–1717) influenced so many people that John Wesley wrote of her: "I know not whether we may not search many centuries to find another woman who was such a pattern of true holiness."[1]

Young Jeanne grew up in France during a time of religious turmoil following the Protestant Reformation. What happened to the Catholic Church after this Luther-led revolution? Certainly a counterrevolution and much fighting occurred. Jeanne Guyon devoted her life to spreading her ideas about the spiritual life, and she infused new life into old, corrupt religious structures. She advocated an inner, contemplative spiritual life rather than outer, tangible works with the motivation of earning one's salvation. She also stressed the importance of prayer and reflection, although she did not neglect social concerns. She merely placed contemplation first in priority.

As was customary in her day, Jeanne married a much older, wealthy man while still in her teens. She was quite unhappy in her marriage, and her only consolation came in her relationship with God. Despite her unhappiness, she remained faithful to her husband and nursed him through years of illness. After they had been married for twelve years, her husband died, leaving her as a widow with two children.

After her husband's death Jeanne seized her newfound freedom and devoted herself to the religious life. Soon she began traveling across France and Switzerland, spreading her ideas about prayer and discovering the depths of Jesus Christ. According to some accounts, people flocked to her for spiritual counsel wherever she went, begging her to teach them how to pray.

Madame Guyon, along with her close friend and follower François de Fénelon, emphasized an interior life of prayer and scripture reading. They were leaders of the Quietist movement in France, a movement whose fundamental principle was its condemnation of all human effort. According to the Quietists, in order to be perfect, a person must annihilate self-will and completely abandon himself or herself to God, even to the extent that that person was no longer concerned about heaven or hell or even about his or her own salvation. Quietism aroused much controversy among church authorities.

Madame Guyon was a prolific writer; among her writings are a 700-page autobiography and a multivolume commentary on scripture. She emphasized becoming united with Christ through silent, contemplative prayer. Because of her mystical ideas, many Catholic leaders viewed her as heretical, condemning her books and called her a dangerous person. Madame Guyon was arrested numerous times and detained at two convents, then later imprisoned in the Bastille for five years. She was forced to sign a retraction of her theories and was asked to refrain from spreading her ideas.

Familiar with suffering and persecution, Jeanne Guyon wrote:

> Be patient in all the suffering that God sends you . . . As soon as anything comes to you in the form of suffering, . . . immediately resign yourself to God. *Accept the matter.* In that moment give yourself up to [God] as a sacrifice. . . .When the cross does arrive in your life, it will not be nearly as burdensome as you first feared.[2]

Jeanne Guyon spent her last years at the estate of her son-in-law. In spite of the retraction she had signed, she continued writing and spreading her ideas about pure love to the end of her life. She died at age sixty-nine, protesting in her will that she had never intended to separate herself from the Catholic Church and stating that she died submissive to the church.

Madame Guyon's ideas did not stop at her death. Her writings soon spread to other countries and became popular with Protestants, particularly in England and Holland.

DAY ONE *From the Shallows to the Depths*

---

*Y*ou may feel that you simply are not one of those people capable of a deep experience with Jesus Christ. Most Christians do not feel that *they* have been called to a deep, inward relationship to their Lord. But we have all been called to the depths of Christ just as surely as we have been called to salvation.

When I speak of this "deep, inward relationship to Jesus Christ," what do I mean? Actually, it is very simple. It is only the turning and yielding of your heart to the Lord. It is the expression of love within your heart for [Christ]. . . .

How then will you come to the Lord to know [Christ] in such a deep way? Prayer is the key. But I have in mind a certain kind of prayer. It is a kind of prayer that is very simple and yet holds the key to perfection and goodness—things found only in God . . . The type of prayer that I have in mind will deliver you from enslavement to every sin. It is a prayer that will release to you every Godly virtue. . . .

May I hasten to say that the kind of prayer I am speaking of is not a prayer that comes from your mind. It is a prayer that begins in the heart. It does not come from your understanding or your thoughts . . . I will go so far as to say that nothing can interrupt this prayer, *the prayer of simplicity.*[3]

I read this excerpt with mixed emotions: desire and despair. Even though I desire to imitate this woman who was so deeply related to God, I despair that I ever will.

I expect that almost everyone can relate to Jeanne's first line. Haven't we all wondered if God especially chooses some people to be saints (or whatever high and holy model we see as too far "out there" to ever attain)? I confess that I feel somewhat this way as I study the lives and writings of the women in this book. I would like to become like them—holy women of the greatest depths of God. And I despair that my "deep, inward relationship" to the Lord is not nearly so deep or inward as I'd like.

Are we *all* called to the depths, as Madame Guyon

says? Yes. Jesus died for this kind of relationship with us. His Spirit lives within each believer, seeking to lead him or her into the depths to experience God in new and healing ways.

How, then, do we move from the shallows to the depths? Through prayer—but not the kind of praying we've always practiced. Not

- "Now I lay me down to sleep"
- liturgical prayers
- pious, wordy prayers
- getting the language right
- claiming the promises in Jesus' name
- formulas like "If you say _____, God has to . . ."

There is much more to prayer than we ever imagined! Prayer can be as simple as a single word like *Help!* It can be as simple as just being alone with nature. It may be spoiled when we try to form thoughts. Prayer is probably best when we rest in an attitude of openness and silently commune with the Lord.

Madame Guyon says the prayer she has in mind holds the key to Christlikeness, deliverance from every kind of sin, and transformation into every godly virtue. Is she arguing against Mass and liturgy when she urges her readers to practice the prayer of simplicity? I don't think so. Her strongest concern is that prayer be real to the person praying—that it be honest and heartfelt.

So? you may be thinking. *I've been praying honest prayers from my heart all my life. What's the difference here?* I believe the difference is a deep, ongoing kind of prayer that underlies every waking activity. More than just an attitude, it is a serene centeredness that holds all of life prayerfully. When you view life from inside this serene and wordlessly prayerful place, you naturally express Christlike virtues in the way you treat people and events. We are not talking simply about a daily prayer time but prayer that is *lived.* In other words, prayer equals life; life equals prayer.

True prayer is not just an add-on to daily living, but it is a life lived out of prayer. It transforms a woman into an image of Christ reflected to all who meet her. Such a woman does not live at a frenetic pace, squeezing a few minutes of God into her day. Rather, she lives from within the prayerful depths of Christ inside her. Madame Guyon reminds us such prayer *is* possible. ◈

Reflection

1. When have you longed for more in your prayer life? Do you desire the "depths"?

2. Have you ever tried just *being* with God without needing words to communicate?

3. Where and how did you learn to pray? What habits do you need to unlearn?

4. When have you given yourself permission to experiment in prayer? What new approach did you try?

5. What sort of prayer that you haven't tried attracts you?

Scripture

Meditate on one or more of these passages:
- Romans 8:26-27, 31-32
- Matthew 6:5-15
- Mark 14:32-42
- John 17
- 2 Peter 1:5-9

Exercise

Deliberately practice some type of prayer other than the norm this week. Consider reading a book on prayer. (See Suggested Reading, page 218.)

Launching Out

I would like to address you as though you were a beginner in Christ, one seeking to know [Christ]. In so doing, let me suggest two ways for you to come to the Lord. I will call the first way "praying the Scripture."

"Praying the Scripture" is a unique way of dealing with the Scripture; it involves both reading and prayer.

Here is how you should begin.

Turn to the Scripture; choose some passage that is simple and fairly practical. Next, come to the Lord. Come quietly and humbly. There, before Him, read a small portion of the passage of Scripture. . . .

Be careful as you read. Take in fully, gently and carefully what you are reading. Taste it and digest it as you read. . . .

You do not move from one passage to another, not until you have *sensed* the very heart of what you have read.

You may then want to take that portion of Scripture that has touched you and turn it into prayer. . . .

"Praying the Scripture" is not judged by *how much* you read but by the *way* in which you read.

If you read quickly, it will benefit you little. You will be like a bee that merely skims the surface of a flower. Instead, in this new way of reading with prayer, you must become as the bee who penetrates into the *depths* of the flower. You plunge deeply within to remove the deepest nectar.[4]

Madame Guyon addresses her readers as beginners, and indeed we all are. Even those who have prayed for decades may feel like babes. Perhaps you haven't encountered this type of prayer. Praying the scripture serves as a wonderful counterbalance to our continual barrage of requests.

Begin by choosing stories of Jesus from the Gospels. Read the story of the crippled woman or the widow who lost her only son. See how tenderly Jesus deals with their deep needs for a healing touch.

As you read the story, imagine the heat of the day and the noise of the crowds. Enter into the setting as if you were the crippled woman and hear Jesus speaking to you. Hear the Lord say to you, "Woman, you are set free from your ailment" (Luke 13:12). Or picture yourself in the place of the widow who had lost her only son, and hear Him say, "Do not weep" (Luke 7:13).

Read the scripture and enter into it as fully as you can. Madame Guyon says, "Take in fully, gently and carefully what you are reading. Taste it and digest it." Let her words become yours. Very slowly, let the words become part of your prayer. "Lord, just as you healed the woman's infirmity, here is mine, in need of your touch."

Our society is so conditioned to instant gratification that praying like this may be a difficult adjustment. We are encouraged to read through the Bible in a year, not to linger over individual words that move us. Perhaps the reason we do not experience God more fully is because we do not slow down long enough for divine presence to permeate our psyches. We cannot allot fifteen minutes a day and command that God fit into our schedules when we are not willing to linger to enjoy that presence when it is given.

Much of the joy of being in God's presence is the slowing of all other senses and luxuriating in that timeless space. Isn't a slower pace what we so value on vacation? Why then do we not avail ourselves of a daily vacation in the presence of our Lord?

Madame Guyon goes on to speak of sensing the essence of the scriptural passage. I have often told my Bible students that we merely skate across the surface of scripture by reading it. To study it, to meditate, and to explore the depths takes more time than we allocate. The plain truth is that we cannot develop a deep relationship with God in just a few minutes a day. I am not sure we can do it even in an hour a day. I aim for an hour a day, but I'd rather have two hours to read, journal, and pray. And I am only scratching the surface. Am I saying that reaching the depths is impossible without living in a convent and doing nothing but reading scripture and praying all day? No. But I am convinced that most Christians devote less daily time to prayer than to deciding what to cook for dinner. And then we expect a vibrant Christian life?

Madame Guyon compares us to bees skimming the surface of a

flower, rather than drinking deeply of the nectar. Just as bees live off the nectar, so we live out of time spent in God's presence.

I prefer the analogy of hummingbirds over Madame Guyon's analogy of bees. When I lived in New York, I hung a hummingbird feeder right outside my kitchen window so that I could see them clearly. One thing I noticed about hummingbirds is that they are totally focused on one goal: getting that nectar. No flitting or dawdling—just drinking deeply, as if their lives depended on it. Likewise, our spiritual lives depend on our drinking deeply of God's Word and praying.

Praying the scriptures gives us another means of incarnating the Word, but praying this way takes more time than reading a one-page devotional or rattling off a rehearsed list of requests to God. Praying the scriptures offers us deep experiences of God's presence. It offers us deep draughts of God's very nature—free for the drinking. ❧

Reflection

1. Have you ever tried praying with scripture? Were you able to savor it slowly?

2. How much difficulty do you have setting aside time and sitting still to meditate on God's Word?

3. What keeps you from spending more time in God's presence? What could you do to remove this barrier?

4. Which kind of bee are you? Why?

5. What do you desire from time spent in God's presence?

Scripture

Read one or more of the following passages, and let it speak to your soul.
- John 15
- Psalm 103
- Psalm 139
- Song of Solomon 2
- Isaiah 40

Exercise

Set aside a block of time (thirty minutes to one hour) when you will not be disturbed. Choose a passage to meditate on, and experiment with this slower pace of reading, then praying over one of the passages listed above. Spend time with whatever word, phrase, or image attracts you. This attraction is the Spirit of God speaking to you individually. Let the Spirit instruct you and usher you into the presence of God.

Internal and External

*Y*our spiritual experiences fall into two categories—those that are external (surface) and those that take place internally, deep within your being. . . .

Your external activities are those which can be seen outwardly. . . . There is no real goodness in them, no spiritual growth in them, and very *little* experience of Christ!

Of course, there is an exception: If your outward actions are a result (a by-product) of something that has taken place deep within you, then these outward actions *do* receive spiritual value and they *do* possess real goodness. . . .

Our way, therefore, is clear. We must give our full attention to those activities that take place deep within our inmost being. *These* are the activities of the Spirit. The Spirit is inward, not outward. . . .

Inward activity begins by simply turning within to Jesus Christ, for that is where He is, within your spirit.

You should be continually turning within to God.

Give [God] all your attention; pour out all the strength of your being purely on Him. . . .

What does it mean to give your whole heart to God? To give your whole heart to God is to have all the energy of your soul always centered on Him.

It is in this way we are conformed to His will.[5]

Madame Guyon makes a sharp distinction between the internal life of prayer and the external life of action on behalf of God's kingdom. She obviously places a higher priority on the prayer life, with the goal of becoming Christlike, than on being busy for God. She claims that activity for God without prayer first is human activity without spiritual value.

For several years, I've had a theory about why so many people today suffer from stress. I believe that we are most stressed when we live only an external life. I don't mean a Christian life compared with an unchristian life, or even a life of prayer compared with a prayerless life. I am speaking of a deeper quality that functions somewhat like an air-traffic controller.

Given daylight or familiarity with the route, most pilots are able to fly perfectly well without guidance from an air-traffic controller. In these conditions pilots can fly entirely by external senses. They can see other planes approaching, the weather, and the runway for landing. Competent pilots are also likely to be able to navigate a flight without help. But this theory assumes that visible (external) factors are the only information the pilot needs.

Madame Guyon's comment on this hypothesis (if she could even conceive of flying) would be an immediate, "But what about the invisible, or internal, factors?" What about the plane coming up behind that's running out of fuel and needs to land first, or the approaching thunderstorm that even the competent pilot can't see—or a host of other factors that only the air-traffic controllers could know?

The air-traffic controller in this analogy is the internal voice of God, which is available to guide our lives around unseen obstacles. An internal life is one lived by listening to the inner voice of the Spirit within—the Holy Spirit, who is our counselor and guide.

Madame Guyon makes a strong statement that our external activities in themselves produce no goodness or spiritual growth and little or no experience of Christ. Wow! What does this say about most of our church programs or about those women who give their lives to supporting church dinners and sitting in the nursery or teaching Sunday school? Do these external activities count for nothing? I believe that Jeanne Guyon would say yes—unless such service results from an inner desire to serve God and the body of Christ.

So is there still a message for us here? I think so. I have been in countless churches (seventy in one year during a year of missionary deputation) where I encountered women who appeared to have substituted being busy with church activities for what Madame Guyon would call an internal life.

I went to these churches longing to talk about how they could impact the world for Jesus. I spoke about mentoring at a women's luncheon almost every Saturday that year. But often the women were talking about crafts, recipes, or family when I so desperately wanted them to see how much they could contribute to the kingdom! They seemed to be stuck when I challenged them to consider what more they could do. When I suggested that they might begin some new work in their communities, their responses were remarkably alike: "Oh, I could never do that!" in an apologetic and helpless tone. They seemed to fear doing anything that moved them from the expected to the substantial. Jeanne Guyon would have some strong words for their hesitance to lead brave lives spawned in the depths of their souls!

So what does the lifestyle of a woman with a rich inner life look like? Perhaps not dramatically different from the women busy with church activity, but look for a subtle difference in the truly rich woman's approach to life. Madame Guyon says that a rich inner life begins by turning within to the Lord, who lives within us. Acts 17:28—"In [God] we live and move and have our being"—aptly describes a rich, inner life.

We could paraphrase this verse by saying, "In the Lord Jesus Christ I live and move and have my being." In Christ I

- determine my time priorities;
- decide on my vocation;
- live as an example before my family, church, and community;
- choose how to use my leisure time;
- determine what kinds of words I speak—encouragement or gossip;
- make value judgments;
- decide how to live my life—whether I listen to the inner voice of Christ or the external voice of society.

Through my smallest decisions I choose who I am becoming every day. Living an inner life means taking the time to pause, go within, and hear the voice of Christ, which then shapes my choices. We don't have to know it all. We simply consult our inner selves, where our "air-traffic controller," the Holy Spirit, is constantly sending signals.

Some of us need to trust our intuition more. I have come to believe that my intuition is the voice of the Holy Spirit for me. My intuition, that inner knowing what is the right course, has never failed me. For some persons, discerning God's voice will require spending more time in the scriptures. But I am absolutely convinced that God is speaking to us constantly, and we choose whether to listen. We all possess the same accessibility to the Spirit and the same number of hours in the day. We can live an internal life "by simply turning to Jesus Christ" and giving the Lord all our attention. We do have a choice. ✍

Reflection

1. Do you live primarily an inner life or an external one? Why?

2. What teaching have you had that helped you make that choice? Which scriptures support both ways?

3. When have you longed for more direction from the Holy Spirit in decision making? What could you do to improve your sensitivity to the Spirit?

4. What keeps you from living a more internal life? What could you do to deepen it?

5. What does it mean for you to give your whole heart to God?

Scripture

Meditate on one or more of these passages:
- Proverbs 23:26
- Psalm 19
- Psalm 119:9-16
- Matthew 15:15-20
- 2 Corinthians 3:2-4

Exercise

On a page of your journal or a large sheet of paper, make two columns headed Internal Activities and External Activities. Think about an average week or month and list every activity in your life in one of those categories.

Look at the external list. What activities could be internalized by simply turning to Jesus before you act? Pray over your life and ask the Spirit to guide you more and more toward an inner life.

Mary or Martha Lifestyle?

*T*he activity of the Spirit must take the place of our own. . . . The outcome will be that, little by little, the activity of God can completely take the place of the activity of the soul.

There is a beautiful example of this in the Gospels. You will recall that Martha was doing something which was very correct, and yet the Lord rebuked her! Why? Because what she was doing, she was doing in her own strength. Martha was not following the moving of the Spirit within her.

You must realize, dear reader, that the soul . . . is naturally restless and turbulent. Your soul accomplishes very little even though it always appears busy.

The Lord answered her, "Martha, Martha, you are worried and distracted by many things; there is need of only one thing. Mary has chosen the better part, which will not be taken away from her" (Luke 10:41-42).

And what had Mary chosen? She had chosen to rest peacefully and tranquilly at the feet of Jesus. She had ceased to live that Christ might be her life!

This illustration highlights just how necessary it is for you to deny yourself and all your activity to follow Jesus Christ. *If you are not led by [the Holy] Spirit, you cannot follow [Jesus].*

When [Christ's] life comes in, your life must be put away. Paul said, "Anyone united to the Lord becomes one spirit with him" (1 Cor. 6:17).[6]

I have always felt sorry for Martha and the reputation she acquired from this passage. She tried to be the perfect hostess. My goodness! She had the Son of God sitting in her living room! Who wouldn't want to fix a nice dinner and offer a place to rest and enjoy friends? And yes, she too wanted to listen to him, but someone had to prepare dinner!

Surely Jesus didn't mean that Martha was wrong to cook dinner and care for his physical needs. So why did he scold her? (For a look at another side to Martha, see John 11:17-27. Jesus knew that Martha was both interested and knowledgeable about theology. They discussed the theology of the resurrection after Lazarus died.) So what was Jesus attempting to teach her (and all of us) on this occasion?

Madame Guyon believed that Jesus' lesson was about the source of our strength. Do we try to get through life by sheer force of our own strength and cry to God for help only when we encounter an impossibility? Unfortunately, most of us live this way. We grow through struggles because we don't depend on God until we admit we have no other choice. "The activity of the Spirit must take the place of our own," Jeanne reminds us.

So how do we allow the Spirit to control our lives? How much does the Spirit do, and how much should we take responsibility for? I've always struggled with this question. Obviously, the Spirit isn't going to cook dinner for my family tonight. What are we to make of this idea that the Spirit's activity must take the place of our own?

Isn't it a question of attitude? I've always loved the verses in scripture about having (or knowing) the mind of Christ. We gain the mind of Christ by spending time at the feet of Christ, as Mary did. She lingered near him, asking questions, listening and learning what was on his mind. It's obvious in this story that Jesus enjoyed Mary's presence, apart from praising her choice of the better use of her time. Spending time with Jesus is always the best use of time—but we can't literally sit at his feet *all* the time. We have laundry to do, children to raise, meals to cook, and other duties waiting for our attendance. But if we have spent time with Jesus first, we can carry that possession of "the mind of Christ" with us into our day's work.

Notice that Jesus scolded Martha for being worried and troubled about too many things—when only one thing was worth that much concern. Mary had chosen to rest peacefully and tranquilly at the feet of Jesus. She had "ceased to live that Christ might be her life."

Jesus knows we must accomplish many things in our day, but we could accomplish them peacefully and tranquilly if we first spent time tuning into the mind of Christ. But I believe there's another truth here for us. Perhaps the balanced life is to be *both* Mary and Martha. Surely none of us is all one or the other. We may tend to be more like one of them and need to pursue some of the other's characteristics. We must pray and work. We must spend time with Jesus and others. Why couldn't our prayer life be as richly developed as our portfolio or our home?

Madame Guyon says, "If you are not led by [the Holy Spirit], you cannot follow [Jesus]." We need to let the Holy Spirit lead us so that we can follow Jesus—wherever that may be. ☙

Reflection

1. Are you more naturally a Mary or a Martha? How did this tendency develop?

2. How do you seek to balance your dominant tendency?

3. What would your life look like if you lived constantly under the Spirit's leadership?

4. How much of the mind of Christ do you possess? Describe what you know of the mind of Christ. Then read 1 Corinthians 2:16.

5. What resistance do you sense in your willingness to be led by the Spirit? How does that resistance manifest itself?

Scripture

Select one or more of the following passages to meditate upon:
- 1 Corinthians 2
- Luke 10:38-42
- Colossians 3:1-17
- Luke 24:44-47
- Philippians 3

Exercise

Memorize Philippians 4:8: "Finally, beloved, whatever is true, whatever is honorable, whatever is just, whatever is pure, whatever is pleasing, whatever is commendable—if there is any excellence and if there is anything worthy of praise, think about these things." Write it on a 3-by-5 card and carry with you to reread until you have it memorized. Then let it reshape your mind like Christ's.

Why Do You Come?

*F*irst of all, come into the Lord's presence by faith. As you are there before [God], keep turning inward to your spirit until your mind is collected and you are perfectly still before [God]. Now, when all your attention is finally turned within and your mind is set on the Lord, simply remain quiet before [God] for a little while.

Perhaps you will begin to enjoy a sense of the Lord's presence. If that is the case, *do not try to think* of anything. Do not try to say anything. Do not try to *do* anything! As long as the sense of the Lord's presence continues, *just remain there.* Remain before [God] exactly as you are.

The awareness of [God's] presence will eventually begin to decrease. When this happens, utter some words of love to the Lord, or simply call on His name. Do this quietly and gently with a believing heart. In so doing, you will once again be brought back to the sweetness of [God's] presence! . . . Once the sweetness of [the Lord's] presence has returned to its fullest, *again* be still before Him. *You should not seek to move as long as He is near.* . . .

Why *do* you come to the Lord? Do you come . . . for the sweetness? Do you come . . . because it is enjoyable to be in the Lord's presence? Let me recommend a higher way.

As you come to the Lord to pray, bring a full heart of pure love, a love that is not seeking anything for itself. Bring a heart that is seeking nothing *from* the Lord, but desires only to please [God] and to do [God's] will. . . . Come just to *please* [the Lord].[7]

I appreciate Madame Guyon's practicality, but sometimes she writes as if mastering these prayer techniques were an automatic reflex! Being able to center and to still your mind is really difficult some days. This morning, I read half of Romans from *The Message* and was ready to pray. Just then the phone rang. Afterward, I simply could not settle my mind again upon learning that my plans for the day had been canceled. I lapsed into a list of prayer requests and lost the serenity that comes from being still and resting in the Lord's presence. Surely it was easier for Jeanne to find quiet time to pray!

I wish Madame Guyon had given more specific ideas at this point about how to still our minds. She tells us to turn inward and assumes that will still us. The presupposition is that our inner selves are not full of turmoil. With our stressful lives, I suspect that it takes us much longer to silence the inner voices demanding our attention.

One way I still my mind is to envision a blank TV screen. Anytime a thought or picture appears on the screen, I picture the screen becoming blank and softly recite "Lord Jesus, Lord Jesus" to refocus. You will need to experiment until you find the least intrusive and most effective means of stilling your busy mind.

When we do "center," it's much easier to think the Lord's thoughts and hear that gentle voice whispering words of love and guidance. Madame Guyon suggests that when we finally arrive in this holy place, we simply sit still and luxuriate in it. Most of us live in such performance-demanding arenas that it sounds too good to be true that we can simply be who we are in the presence of the Lord. Plus, we've been so indoctrinated in formulas for prayer—"Do this and say that" for prayer to "work." But prayer is *not* about formulas. Instead, Madame Guyon gives us these instructions:

- Don't try to think anything.
- Don't try to say anything.
- Don't try to do anything.
- Rest in the Lord's presence for as long as it continues.

What a relief! How restful it sounds to simply *be* in the Lord's presence and enjoy sweetness and rest. No formulas, no demands. Jeanne Guyon asks us: Why do you come to prayer at all? Is it for the sweetness and because it's so enjoyable? Or is it only to please your Lord?

I confess that I am hooked on the joy of being in the Lord's presence. I love Sundays—how wonderful to be commanded to take a day off! Furthermore, I love the rest and the freedom I enjoy simply being in the Lord's presence for fellowship. I don't make long prayer lists any more. I bring myself and all those I love and for whom I feel concern to the Lord. Whether I list all those concerns is not important, for the matter of utmost importance is that I commune with the Lord and that I become empowered and enriched by that communion. But the danger for me is that I expect to feel good about every prayer time and feel cheated on days when I don't leave that hour feeling blessed and loved. Even prayer for the sake of the Lord's presence doesn't seem to be enough.

Madame Guyon says that when we come to the Lord, we must bring a heart full of love and a desire to please God. How often I need to be reminded that it's not about me! Rather, it's all about our gracious Lord and how we offer our praise and love. Madame Guyon writes, "Bring a heart that is seeking nothing *from* the Lord, but desires only to please [God] and to do [God's] will."

We are such self-absorbed creatures that it's difficult even to imagine prayer that is not asking God for something we want. Our skewed thinking perverts worship into nonstop requests. We may need to reevaluate our prayer times and substitute worship for requests, which frees us to come to prayer just so we can please God. ❧

Reflection

1. Do you have a quiet place where you can commune with the Lord undisturbed? If not, where might you create such a place?

2. How long does it usually take to still your mind to pray? How do you still your mind?

3. How do you usually notice the Lord's presence? What is your response?

4. How hard is it for you to simply rest in that presence, rather than feeling you must do or say something to impress the Lord?

5 Can you simply spend time in the Lord's presence without asking for anything for yourself?

Scripture

Read and meditate on one or more of the following passages:
- Revelation 3:20-22
- Revelation 5:11-14
- Psalm 66:1-7
- Isaiah 28:23, 29

Exercise

Practice prayerfully sitting for ten minutes each day—just *being* and focusing on the Lord. Think of it as rest or prayer or discipline—whatever helps you break your compulsive need to perform for the Lord, as opposed to letting God love you.

Come As a Weak Child

*A*s you come to [God], come as a weak child, one who is all soiled and badly bruised—a child that has been hurt from falling again and again. Come to the Lord as one who has no strength of [her] own; come to [God] as one who has no power to cleanse [herself]. . . . Humbly lay your pitiful condition before your Father's gaze. . . .

Come to [God], then, as a sheep who is looking to [her] shepherd for . . . *real* food. As You come to [the Lord], utter something like this: "Oh, loving Shepherd, You feed Your flock with Yourself, and You are really my daily bread." . . .

Dear child of God, all your concepts of what God is like really amount to nothing. Do not try to imagine what God is like. Instead, simply believe in [God's] presence. Never try to imagine what God will do. There is no way God will ever fit into your concepts. What then shall you do? Seek to behold Jesus Christ by looking to Him in your inmost being, in your spirit. . . .

You may come to the Lord by looking to [Jesus] as your Physician. Bring to Him all your sicknesses so that He can heal them. But as you come to Him, do not come with anxiety or restlessness. And as you come, pause from time to time. This period of waiting silently before the Lord will gradually *increase!* . . .

When the presence of the Lord really becomes your experience, you will actually discover that you have gradually begun to love this silence and peaceful rest which come with [the Lord's] presence.[8]

In this excerpt Madame Guyon gives us three pictures of God to hold in our minds as we pray.

First, *God is a loving parent to the orphaned.* We should come to our heavenly Father as a weak child, bruised from falling and possessing no strength of our own. That should not be hard for us to imagine.

I have often felt like a frightened child—powerless to change my circumstances or heal my own hurts. When my first husband abandoned me and left me with a five-month-old daughter, I knew a desperation that either depended on the Lord or gave up on life. In fact, I thought my life was over—at age twenty-four. I thought no man would ever want me again and that all my dreams of entering the ministry were lost. I got on my knees and asked the Lord to heal my bruised heart and shattered dreams. It's a long story, but God redemptively answered my prayers. I returned to college, went on to seminary, and there met the man of my dreams with whom I have ministered for the last twenty years. As Madame Guyon counsels us, humbly I laid my "pitiful condition before [the] Father's gaze," and He had mercy on me.

Her second picture of God is that of *the Shepherd who offers real food.* The real food is the nourishment of divine presence within us, which satisfies like nothing else can. We can be bone weary and desperate for refreshing. We can come empty of everything except our petitions or loneliness or fear or whatever and find plenteous sufficiency for all our needs. Lavish love, great grace, and substantial soul food for our every need are available merely by coming into the presence of our loving Shepherd.

I love the passage in Ezekiel 34 that tells of the false and true shepherds. The false shepherds in this analogy symbolize the priests of Israel who have neglected God's people. God, the great shepherd, offers love and care to us. The good shepherd will

- rescue the sheep from all the places they have scattered,
- tend them in rich pastures,
- search for the lost and bring back the strays,
- bind up the injured sheep,
- strengthen the weak sheep,
- shepherd the flock with justice,
- save the flock so that they will no longer be plundered,
- make a covenant of peace and rid the land of wild beasts so they can live in safety. (See Ezek. 34:11 and following.)

"They shall know that I, the LORD their God, am with them, and that they, the house of Israel, are my people, says the Lord GOD. You are my sheep, the sheep of my pasture and I am your God, says the Lord GOD" (Ezek. 34:30-31).

The third picture of our God is as *the Healer to whom we can bring all our sicknesses.* We can approach God in confidence with no anxiety. Why? Because the Healer loves to heal us. We simply need to come and wait silently, holding our needs lightly in prayerful, uplifted hands. But beware, God does not always heal us as we would expect or even like. Our confidence comes not from knowing that we will get what we want, but that we will get what is best—true wholeness.

Madame Guyon warns us not to imagine, to predict, or try to control what God will do with us. How can a child tell a parent what is best, or a sheep direct the shepherd to the best pasture? Today's meditation is about learning to loosen our control on God and on our dearest wishes. We normally go to God (a God we have imagined a certain way) and instruct God what to do, because we think our way is best. Madame Guyon warns us that we are playing God—not praying—when we do this. Real faith and real prayer come from the helpless, not those in control. We must remember the truth of this maxim: "There is a God and it is *not* me."

Come to God in your weakness. Sit in silence and let the Holy One heal you and shepherd you as only God can and does. Learn to let God be God. ❧

Reflection

1. What is your image of God? What picture do you have in your mind as you pray?

2. What images and understandings of God might you "unlearn" and replace with an image or understanding such as the ones Madame Guyon describes?

3. Which of these images for God appeals to you most—loving parent, shepherd, or physician? Why?

4. What are you holding in your hands that you are not willing to cede to God's control?

5. What in you hurts or needs healing right now? Share it with your Shepherd.

Scripture

Read and meditate on one or more of these passages:

- Psalm 23
- Ezekiel 34
- Matthew 8:1-17
- Matthew 9:18-34
- John 10:1-8

Exercise

Spend some time meditating on Ezekiel 34. Have you encountered any false shepherds who made it hard for you to believe in God's love for you?

What characteristic of God, the Good Shepherd, is most meaningful to you and why?

Distractions

Once your heart has been turned inwardly to the Lord, you will have an impression of His presence. You will be able to notice His presence more acutely because your outer senses have now become very calm and quiet. Your attention is no longer on outward things or on the surface thoughts of your mind; instead, sweetly and silently, your mind becomes occupied with what you have read and by that touch of His presence. . . .

What about distractions?

Let us say your mind begins to wander. Once you have been deeply touched by the Lord's Spirit and are distracted, be diligent to bring your wandering mind back to the Lord. This is the easiest way in the world to overcome external distractions.

When your mind has wandered, don't try to deal with it by changing what you are thinking. You see, if you pay attention to what you are thinking, you will only irritate your mind and stir it up more. Instead, *withdraw* from your mind! Keep turning within to the Lord's presence. By doing this you will win the war with your wandering mind and yet never directly engage in the battle! . . .

The Lord's chief desire is to reveal [the divine self] to you and, in order for [the Lord] to do that, He gives you abundant grace. The Lord gives you the experience of enjoying His presence. He touches you, and His touch is so delightful that, more than ever, you are drawn inwardly to [God].[9]

I am constantly amazed at how many irrelevant things come to mind when I begin to pray: Tasks I need to complete today, conversations, or situations suddenly flood my empty thought spaces. Just when I think I've quieted my spirit and am truly ready to pray, I am ambushed by distracting thoughts.

Madame Guyon gives lengthy instructions about quieting our hearts before God. She suggests gently waiting before the Lord with our minds turned toward our spirits, where the Lord is found. She calls the inner recesses of our beings the "Holy of Holies," where we dwell with God. She invites us to this place to pray.

Jeanne describes this inner space in each of us as calm and quiet. We reach this place by focusing on our inner world and ignoring outer surroundings. (I do this best by being in the dark or covering my eyes with my hands so that I can't see anything around me. I fight distractions by trying to lose visual contact with my immediate surroundings.) "Sweetly and silently, your mind becomes occupied with what you have read [scripture] and that touch of His presence," she says.

Stilling your soul and quieting your mind may sound too time consuming or like too much trouble if it is a new concept for you. Actually, one experience of getting quiet enough to truly sense the presence of the Lord is sufficient to get hooked. It takes only a few times of disciplining our minds (this is really all it is) before we've made it a habit to begin our prayer times by "centering," or focusing our thoughts on God.

Once we have quieted our minds and let go of thoughts clamoring for our attention, we are ready to pray. Some days, we will find it exceedingly satisfying—so much so that we will not want to leave the Lord's presence. But other days distractions will plague us. How do we get rid of them?

Madame Guyon says it doesn't help to get frustrated or to try frontal attacks on distracting thoughts. You may have heard the suggestion to keep a pad of paper handy and write memos of the intruding thoughts that must be dealt with later. Jeanne suggests another strategy for reclaiming inner quiet. She believed the key was to ignore the distractions and refocus on the Lord—concentrating on what you desire to think of, rather than on what you don't. She promises this technique will win the war against distractions. The entire process involves learning to bring our minds under subjection to the Lord until quieting becomes a disciplined habit.

And the reward? Madame Guyon writes, "The Lord's chief desire is to reveal [the divine self] to you." Is this too good to be true? No. God desires an intimate relationship with us so much that the Lord gives abundant grace to discipline our unruly minds. And when we have done that, Madame Guyon reminds us, God will touch us. That touch will delight us and draw us close to our gracious Creator. It's a cycle of loving communion—God gives us grace to conquer distractions. When we apply that grace, God allows us to experience divine presence, which in turn, draws us even closer. And then, the more we know of God, the more we want to know. The cycle never ends, even in eternity.

Reflection

1. How do you begin your prayer times? In what ways do you attempt to quiet your mind and spirit?

2. What atmosphere or quieting strategy works best for you?

3. What thoughts usually distract you? Work? Family? Things to do? How do you deal with distractions?

4. What do you think the Lord might want to reveal to you?

5. Think about a time when you have experienced divine presence.

Scripture

Read and meditate on one or more of the following:
- Isaiah 30:15 and 32:17
- Psalm 16:11
- Psalm 131
- Zephaniah 3:17

Exercise

In your prayer times this week, focus on quieting (centering) your soul. You might want to imagine a peaceful empty landscape. Then picture the Lord walking toward you; consider what the two of you might talk about.

Periods of Dryness

*D*ear reader, you must realize that God has only one desire. Certainly you can never understand a dry spell unless you understand what [God's] desire is. [God's] desire is to give Himself to the soul that really loves Him. . . . *And yet* it is true that this God who desires to give Himself to you will often conceal Himself from you—from you, the very one who seeks Him!

Now why would God do that? Dear saint of God, you must learn the ways of your Lord. Yours is a God who often hides Himself. He hides Himself for a purpose. Why? *His purpose is to rouse you from spiritual laziness.* His purpose in removing Himself from you is to cause you to pursue Him.

The Lord Jesus is looking about everywhere for that Christian who will remain faithful and loving even when [God] has withdrawn Himself. If the Lord finds such a faithful soul, when He does return, He rewards the faithfulness of His child. He pours out upon that faithful one abundant goodness and tender caresses of love. . . .

You must await the return of your Beloved with *patient love.* Join with that love *self-denial* and *humiliation!* Even though the Lord has hidden Himself, remain constantly before Him. There before Him, pour out your love upon Him passionately and yet, I would add, always peacefully. . . .

What if the Lord called upon you to spend *your whole lifetime* waiting for His return to you?. . .What *would* you do?[10]

Have you noticed that these women saints never deal with the easy stuff? They ask their readers hard questions and demand no less than our best. Here Jeanne deals with one of the hardest aspects of the Christian life: God's absence. No, God is never truly absent, but sometimes we feel as if God has abandoned us.

Jeanne minces no words in explaining why we must endure dry times spiritually: to wake us from our slothful slumber. As long as our relationship with God is flowing smoothly, we can coast spiritually and enjoy the ride. We become complacent about our (slow) spiritual

progress. We usually feel quite proud of ourselves for being such wonderful Christian examples! Never mind that nothing new has happened
in us spiritually in quite some time; perhaps we are boring both God
and ourselves. So our loving Lord quietly withdraws to see how long it
will take us to notice the absence and to pine for that precious presence.

I do not want to leave the impression that I (or any Christian) feel
the presence of the Lord in every quiet time. That's not humanly possible. And yet, even when I don't hear any special word from the Lord,
I have a sense of communing with God. But in a dry spell, that sense
of communion may disappear altogether. I may lose interest in praying
and find excuses to shorten that time, or else I fume, blaming God for
not coming to meet me. My "quiet" time becomes rather noisy as I
fuss at God—mainly because I can't leave this time with good feelings.

Madame Guyon tells us that the purpose of God's withdrawal is to
cause us to pursue the Lord with even more desire. God longs for us
to come to a time of prayer eagerly hungering for divine presence, not
simply to fulfill a Christian duty. So God withdraws, leaving us to pursue our heart's desire, fulfillment by God alone. Nothing else will fill
this void in us.

But sometimes learning this lesson takes us a long, lonely time.
After we've tried everything else, we finally turn inward to the
dwelling place of God, deep within us.

But what if after we finally turn toward the Lord, we still experience God's absence? We, the ones who have become lazy and inatten-
tive, simply await God's return. Now we must stay alert and listen for
the return of the Beloved (like the lover in Song of Solomon).
Madame Guyon says that this waiting demonstrates that we are waiting for God alone, not for the "good feelings" of God's presence or for
any answered prayers—but for the joy of communion.

So how long could I wait for God to return? I hope never to be so
tested. And what if I had to wait the rest of my life? I shudder even to
think of it. But I have endured a couple of waits that lasted months,
one in the last two years. I waited in trusting expectation, daily hoping

that this would be the day of Jesus' return. Surely waiting is life's hardest task!

Even now I am waiting on my college-aged daughter, Elizabeth, to arrive from five hundred miles away. I can do nothing to hurry her return to me but must wait until she arrives at the door. It's the same with the Lord's return. God knows what is best for me, and when I can wait no longer, God will come to me—

"And the joy we share as we tarry there, none other has ever known."[11]

Reflection

1. How would you describe your own spiritual apathy? What rouses you from periods of spiritual sloth?

2. How do you respond once you recognize these times?

3. How long has it been since you encountered a spiritual dry spell? How did you handle it?

4. What does pursuing the Lord look like in your spiritual life?

5. How long are you willing to wait for the return of the Lord's presence? What helps you as you wait?

Scripture

Select one or more of the following passages and meditate on it:
- Song of Solomon 3:1-4
- Psalm 27
- Psalm 51:11-19
- Luke 24:13-35
- 1 Thessalonians 5:1-11

Exercise

Sit down with your journal and take a spiritual inventory. What are your regular spiritual practices? Which ones might you discard for now? What new spiritual disciplines might you incorporate to good effect? Note what you think are the causes of spiritual boredom or slippage in discipline. Sit prayerfully with the inventory and ask the Lord to help you discern God's good pleasure in your spiritual progress.

Love the Cross

*I*f you gave yourself to [the Lord] to be *blessed* and to be *loved*, you cannot suddenly turn around and take back your life at another season . . . when you are being *crucified!*

Nor will you find any comfort from [other people] when you have been put on the cross. Any comfort that comes to you when you are knowing the cross comes to you from the Lord.

You must learn to love the cross. [The person] who does not love the cross does not love the things of God (Matthew 16:23). It is impossible for you to truly love the Lord without loving the cross. The believer who loves the cross finds that even the bitterest things that come [her] way are sweet. . . .

How much do you desire to hunger after God? You will hunger after God, and find [God], in the same proportion that you hunger after the cross. . . .

. . . God gives us the cross, and then the cross gives us God. . . .

Then how will you treat suffering? Or, to put it another way, how do you respond to the Lord's working of the cross in your life?

You respond this way. As soon as anything comes to you in the form of suffering, . . . immediately resign yourself to God. *Accept the matter.* In that moment give yourself up to [the Lord] as a sacrifice.[12]

These are not the words we want to hear. Loving the cross sounds, at first, like an easy and sentimental thing to do. But not by Jeanne Guyon's definition! To love the cross is to embrace suffering, she says. And she should know about suffering, since she spent nearly twenty years in prison or in exile.

But *embrace* suffering? Most of us avoid suffering at all costs. Our culture tells us we don't have to suffer — that we will find a way out if only we look hard enough or pay enough money. But our culture sells us a lie. Even Christians cannot avoid suffering in this life. There is simply no formula for avoiding it. So we had better learn how to deal with suffering and save the energy we waste on pretending.

Madame Guyon knew human nature well. We want to come to God to be "blessed and loved." We who have been blessed assume that God's job is to continue blessing us. We think that being blessed does not include any suffering. Some people have erroneously taught that God loves us too much to ever let us suffer. But consider this concept from a biblical standpoint. Did God *not* love Jesus when He was suffering on the cross? Suffering is a part of life because of sin. Jesus died to overcome sin's dominion in the world. In the meantime, we'd better listen to Madame Guyon and learn to love the cross.

So just what would loving the cross look like in our lives? Jill, my spiritual director, taught me that the best way (notice that I did not say the painless way) to get through suffering is to meet it head-on—to embrace it—and attempt to see what the experience can teach us. We shouldn't pretend when we're suffering. Instead, we say to God and to ourselves: *I am hurting. I am suffering, and I need help to deal with this reality.* Then we discover—like Shadrach, Meshach, and Abednego in the fiery furnace—that God is present with us in our suffering!

Jesus knows what it means to suffer alone, and he wants to spare us that agony of loneliness. He may not miraculously remove us from the hurtful situation, but he comes to transform it. Remember what happened to the three in the furnace? They came out without even an odor of smoke, let alone injury!

When God comes to be with us in our suffering, we can take our focus off the suffering and look at God. Madame Guyon expresses it like this: "Even the bitterest things that come [our] way are sweet." Why? Not because suffering is less painful, but because the presence of the Lord sweetens that shared bitterness.

Then Jeanne compares our desire for God to our desire for the cross. No, we needn't search for suffering; plenty of suffering exists in this needy world without that. Rather, we care about the things of God. Is God concerned about murder? Does the Lord weep over AIDS deaths? Does God call us to weep over the suffering of displaced and hungry children? Yes. These are some of the corporate sins Jesus died for and the sins over which God still weeps.

Personal suffering *will* come our way. And when it does, how should we meet it? Madame Guyon gives this advice: "Immediately resign yourself to God. *Accept the matter.* In that moment give yourself up to [God] as a sacrifice." She clearly calls us to face suffering.

We shouldn't whine or rail, "Why did God allow this to happen to me?" Instead, we offer our suffering to God, trusting that it will be used for the kingdom's glory.

We must learn to see life and suffering from God's perspective. We must learn to love the cross.

✑

Reflection

1. What have you been taught about God's love and providence for your life?

2. What might your hunger (or lack of hunger) for the cross say about your love for God?

3. How often do you weep over the sufferings of others in our world?

4. What are you suffering now and how are you dealing with it? How might you embrace suffering and offer yourself to God as a sacrifice?

5. How have you begun to love the cross?

Scripture

Read and meditate on any of the following passages:
- Daniel 3
- John 19
- Matthew 26
- Psalm 22

Exercise

Meditatively read about the Lord's suffering in John 19 or Matthew 26. Let yourself truly feel the suffering and what loving the cross meant for Jesus. Then write in your journal changes that might take place in your life if you attempted to love the cross of Jesus.

Divine Uniformity

*Y*ou begin at conversion with *self-activity*. But gradually, although progressively, you move toward *passivity*. Along the way between these two points your soul is gradually purified of all those movements of the soul that are so distinguishable and full of so much variety. . . .

Your capacity for becoming passive is gradually increased. Your capacity to be passive before God and under the crushing of the cross . . . is enlarged in a secret, hidden manner.

You are now passing through the first stage of being drawn into the depths of God. He is *conforming* you to His purity.

But there are two stages in God's drawing you. The second stage is *uniformity* with God. . . .

Self-effort gradually decreases. Eventually, it ceases altogether. When self-effort ceases, your will is passive before God.

You have come to uniformity.[13]

I am struggling right now with the tension between self-activity and passivity before God. I am attempting to begin a new ministry and am greatly aware of the need to become visible in a new place. At the same time, I fear running ahead of God.

My natural inclinations are to wait until God acts to ensure that God's initiative establishes my ministry. But then I get impatient and feel the need to make things happen if God doesn't do it quickly enough. When I read this excerpt from Jeanne, she seemingly affirms my instinct to wait—but "How long, O Lord" must I wait?

Self-activity comes so naturally to most of us that we never even give it a thought. The problem develops when activity precedes prayer. In the last three years I've become obsessed with praying for discernment of God's will. Unfortunately, I still don't feel I've learned much. My only encouragement is that Madame Guyon does say that this ability to remain passive grows gradually.

Why is it so hard for us to remain passive and wait on God to act? I have two questions: How much do I do, and how much does God do?

One thing I have discovered is that if I feel that I *must* act, then the feeling probably originated with me and not God, since I tend to be somewhat urgency-oriented. Over the years, I have noticed that God rarely acts out of a sense of urgency or speed. God's direction is much more likely to come softly, yet repeatedly, over a long period of time. This fits with Jeanne Guyon's concept of passivity, for passivity is receptive, not reactive.

Another consideration for me is this: What motivates my feeling that I need to act immediately? If I am feeling urgent, I am most likely trying to fix something God has been too slow on (in my "wise" estimation). Not many things are urgent. In fact, the most important things in our lives rarely shout at us to act immediately. Relationships, self-care, and quality time with God aren't about urgency but consistency. Our frenetic culture, though, tells us to hurry.

So Jeanne advises us to become more passive—to be more receptive and drawn to a greater extent into the depths of God. As this happens, she says we are purified and ultimately united with God. I am not even sure I know what it means to be united with God, but I long to find out. And Madame Guyon says the way to find out is to become more passive. For me, I guess this means waiting a little longer before I give up on a ministry and take the first job I find—which of course I don't want to do, but waiting is so hard!

Madame Guyon says self-effort gradually ceases. I guess I still have a long way to go. ❧

Reflection

1. How would you describe your spiritual journey—as active or passive?

2. How do you respond to the thought of being passive?

3. What part of you needs to be conformed to God's purity?

4. What appeals to you about the thought of union with God?

5. What current situation is creating tension between wanting to wait on God and wanting to fix it yourself?

Scripture

Read and meditate on one or more of these passages:
- Philippians 2:1-2
- Psalm 27:14
- Psalm 130:5
- Acts 1:4
- Titus 2:13

Exercise

In your journal, list situations you are asking the Lord to resolve. Make one column of situations, another column of your actions if you tried to fix them, and a blank column to record God's resolutions. Experiment with waiting on the Lord, and see for yourself the value of such waiting.

I fully realize that

there was nothing about me

which could have claimed

[God's] divine attention;

anything which is good in me

is the effect of

[God's] mercy—

that and nothing else.

—THÉRÈSE OF LISIEUX

Meet Thérèse of Lisieux

We become acquainted with Saint Thérèse of the Child Jesus (1873–1897) through her autobiography, *The Story of a Soul*. Thérèse wrote her life story in obedience to the request of her sister, Pauline, who was also her mother superior at the Carmelite convent in Lisieux, France.

The Story of a Soul is not a continuous story but is instead a collection of three letters written at different times to different people. The first letter was written between January 1895 and January 1896 and addressed to Mother Agnes (her sister Pauline). Thérèse wrote the second letter in three days, between September 13–16, 1896, and addressed it to Sister Marie of the Sacred Heart (her oldest sister Marie). The final part is a notebook that Thérèse wrote between June and September 1896 and addressed to the Reverend Mother Marie de Gonzague. By the time she wrote this part of her autobiography, Thérèse was an invalid who spent long afternoons sitting in a wheelchair under chestnut trees. By the first part of July, she had grown so weak that she had to finish writing in pencil. The pencil literally fell from her hand as she wrote the last word, *love*. Not long after that Thérèse died.

The Story of a Soul was published in 1898, one year after Thérèse's death. The nuns at Carmel Convent wondered how they could ever deplete their stock of two thousand copies. However, soon the convent began receiving letters of inquiry about the book, up to five hundred a day! Thérèse's humble story sold 47,000 copies during its first twelve years of publication. Today millions of copies of her autobiography have been sold.

Perhaps you wonder what makes this autobiography so special. Thérèse herself. Her entire life, from earliest awareness on, was aimed toward entering the convent at Lisieux, her hometown. She entered the convent at age fifteen, joining three of her sisters in holy matrimony to the church. (Eventually all five girls in her family became nuns.)

I think two virtues especially characterize Thérèse: (1) humility and (2) a consuming desire to be holy and to please God. Her humility is reflected in the first part of her autobiography, titled "The Story of a Little White Flower." This concept arose from Thérèse's meditation on the beauty of the wildflowers in a meadow. She mused that surely all of the flowers would like to be roses and thereby offer more praise to God. But then where would we be without violets and daisies? Thérèse compared these flowers to saints. Surely all of us long to be great saints, she says, but God made lesser saints as well. Thus she counted herself as a small flower—a lesser saint who gave pleasure to God by her humble, unremarkable life (from her perspective). Thérèse lived to obey Christ and become whatever God desired. I find her simple desire to please God and her humility appealing.

The first half of Thérèse's autobiography focuses on her childhood years and her relationship with her sisters and father. Despite the fact that her mother died when Thérèse was only four, Thérèse recalls a happy home life and God's total integration in it. The youngest child and often sickly, Thérèse was pampered. She mentions her being spoiled as if she were fully aware of it as a child. Yet it sounds as if loving and being loved made up her whole existence. Deeply aware of her weaknesses, Thérèse seldom needed correction. The thought of disappointing her beloved family kept her true to their and her convictions.

As Thérèse grew older, so grew her desire to enter the Carmel Convent in Lisieux. She didn't want to join the convent just to be near her "dear mother," as she called her sister Pauline. She longed for nothing more than to give her future to her Lord.

Thérèse badgered the bishop and even petitioned the pope to let her enter the convent early. Finally she received permission at age fifteen.

Thérèse's chapters about her life in the convent deal mainly with her perceived failings. A perfectionist by nature, she never felt satisfied that she had performed purely enough.

One day a sister nun surprised Thérèse by saying to her, "Dear child, I can't imagine you have a great deal to confide to your superiors."

When Thérèse asked why she would say such a thing, the nun replied, "Why, there's such a simplicity about your soul. Of course, the nearer you approach perfection, the simpler you will become; nearness to God always makes us simple."[1]

Thérèse was a simple person, but she continued to agonize over her minutest failure to love her Lord and those around her perfectly. As she said, "I care for nothing, I want nothing, except to do what Jesus wants."[2] And that she did.

Reading Thérèse's story inspires pure joy—the same simple joy in life, in nature and all beautiful things around her, and primarily in her Lord. Her life was characterized by joy, despite years of illness and ultimately the limitations of an invalid. She used her twenty-four short years on earth to practice holiness for an eternity that was very real to her.

In 1997 Pope John Paul II declared Thérèse a Doctor of the Church. She is the youngest person and one of three women (all of whom are discussed in this book) to be honored with this title.

What can we learn from this humble soul? Many things, but perhaps the most important is a simple joy in living with the Lord.

Of Flowers and Saints

I realised, then, that all the flowers [God] has made are beautiful; the rose in its glory, the lily in its whiteness, don't rob the tiny violet of its sweet smell, or the daisy of its charming simplicity. I saw that if all these lesser blooms wanted to be roses instead, nature would lose the gaiety of her springtide dress—there would be no little flowers to make a pattern over the countryside. And so it is with the world of souls, which is [God's] garden. [God] wanted to have great Saints, to be his lilies and roses, but he has made lesser Saints as well; and these lesser ones must be content to rank as daisies and violets, lying at his feet and giving pleasure to his eye like that. Perfection consists simply in doing [God's] will, and being just what [God] wants us to be.

This, too, was made clear to me—that our Lord's love makes itself seen quite as much in the simplest of souls as in the most highly gifted, as long as there is no resistance offered to his grace. After all, the whole point of love is making yourself small.[3]

Thérèse's childlike spirit shines through in her autobiography as she writes of the simplest everyday things. She finds awe and wonder in everything God made. She sees all things in life as symbols of Jesus' love for us. Seeing Jesus in creation is one of her favorite topics. And it seems she particularly loved flowers because she mentions them often. Who besides Thérèse would equate saints with wildflowers?

Thérèse's obsession with beauty appeals greatly to me. I love all things beautiful, especially flowers. I remember the long, dreary winters during the three years we lived in Scotland. Gray days that seemed to last forever were brightened by the arrival of daffodils in late January. No, the daffodils weren't blooming yet. They arrived in the flower shops from Holland. Europeans are obsessed with having fresh flowers in the house year-round. We were poor students who couldn't afford fresh flowers, but the daffodils were cheap, and I learned to anticipate their arrival in January. The dark days of January were brightened every time I looked at my floral sunshine. Daffodils are still some of my favorite flowers, reminding me of the resurrection of the earth after winter freezes.

Roses, however, would be the epitome of the flower hierarchy for most people. No wonder Thérèse honors them by comparing them with the "great Saints." Roses can move me to tears with their layers of fragrant, velvety beauty. I often examine rose petals and wonder what God makes the petals out of. I can't look at a rose without a sense of wonder about a God who could make something so beautiful. After all, what is the purpose of a flower except for our enjoyment? Surely a God who would make a rose must be a God of love and beauty.

Certainly Thérèse saw her Lord in flowers and every other aspect of creation. But what about Thérèse's idea that we are God's garden? She asserts that God has made each of us a certain type of flower to complete the variety and beauty of some heavenly design. Are we content with our floral designation in the Master's plan?

I imagine myself as a purple pansy. I love the tenacity of pansies. They bloom early and for a long time, since they don't mind the cold. I would want to be as faithful to my Lord as pansies, which aren't destroyed by cooler temperatures. And purple? Purple is such an intense color—there is nothing insipid or undecided about deep purple. So would I long to be as intensely devoted to my heavenly Gardener.

Most people wouldn't consider the pansy as valuable as a rose, but pansies provide me as much joy with their intense color and longevity. But another intimation in Thérèse's flower analogy is that we should not compare ourselves: pansies with roses or violets with daisies. She says God has a pattern in mind for the whole of creation—or in our case, the church. All of us help complete the work of the kingdom. Each flower pleases God, becoming part of the overall effect of the garden.

Our difficulty, then, is to be content with being just one small flower in God's great garden. We long to be the outstanding rose that everyone will admire. But Thérèse knew that all flowers are equally pleasing to God, and God is the one we should most desire to please. The other flowers are not our concern. She advises us to concentrate on "lying at his feet and giving pleasure to his eye." "Perfection," Thérèse says, "consists simply in doing [God's] will and being just what [God] wants us to be." Pleasing God ought to be our greatest concern in life. Indeed, this was true of Thérèse; giving pleasure to God defined her life.

Thérèse's last thought convicts me—that God's love will be clearly seen in me as long as I do not resist the Lord's grace. I am not even sure how I resist grace, yet I have longed and begged for more grace in my life. I know when I am not "graced" (gracious), but I never *intend* to resist grace. I feel it more as a lack than a resistance. Thérèse challenges me to probe deeper into my soul and learn how not to resist grace so that the Lord's love may shine more clearly through me. ❧

Reflection

1. What sort of flower do you imagine yourself to be in God's garden? Which one would you like to be?

2. How often do you compare yourself to other, "more beautiful" Christians? Why?

3. How does your life offer a sweet-smelling aroma to God? How might you encourage that fragrance?

4. Can you be content with the part God has given you in the design of the kingdom?

5. In what ways do you resist God's grace? How do you access it?

Scripture

Read and meditate on any of these passages:
- 2 Corinthians 2:14-17
- Psalm 141
- Psalm 64
- 1 Corinthians 15:9-11
- 2 Corinthians 9:6-15

Exercise

Sit near a beautiful flower and enjoy it for a while. Examine it, smell it, feel it, and let the wonder of the flower fill you with awe at the love of a Creator who would create such a work of beauty. Then ask the Lord to show you what kind of flower you were designed to be and how you might give pleasure to your Creator. Record your thoughts in your journal.

The Little Flower

*I*t's for you [Thérèse's sister Pauline] only that I mean to write down the story of the little flower Jesus has picked. . . .

If a wild flower could talk, I imagine it would tell us quite candidly about all God has done for it; there would be no point in hushing up his gifts to it, out of mock humility and pretending that it was ugly, that it had no smell, that the sun had robbed it of its bloom, or the wind broken its stem, knowing that all that wasn't true. Anyhow, this isn't going to be the autobiography of a flower like that. On the contrary, I'm delighted to be able to put them on record, the favours our Lord has shown me, all quite undeserved. I fully realise that there was nothing about me which could have claimed [God's] divine attention; anything which is good in me is the effect of [God's] mercy—that and nothing else.

It was [God] that chose the soil I was to grow in—holy ground, all steeped (you might say) in the scent of purity. He saw to it that eight lilies of dazzling whiteness should grow up there before me. Even so, his little flower must be lovingly protected from the pestilential airs of worldliness; he would transplant it, when its petals were only just beginning to open, to Mount Carmel—a place perfumed already by the scent of two lilies that had blessed her spring-tide with their gentle companionship. It is seven years now since that flower took root in the garden where the Lover of Souls had planted it; and now there are *three* lilies to lift their heads close by; a fourth is unfolding, still under the watchful care of Jesus, not far away.[4]

Knowing some of Thérèse's background can help us decode this excerpt. The eight flowers represent all her family members (though they were all alive together only a short time). The two lilies at Carmel are her sisters Pauline and Marie. They arrived at the convent before Thérèse, and Celine, her youngest sister, was the "fourth . . . unfolding" because she had not yet entered the convent.

Thérèse called herself the "little flower Jesus has picked." This quotation occurs on the page after her analogy of our being flowers in God's garden. She caricatures herself as a little flower Jesus has picked for his pleasure (implied) as a means to tell of God's favors to her.

What fresh metaphors she uses! "If a wild flower could talk, I imagine it would. . . ." Again we see an example of her playfulness and unrestrained joy in creation. Also notice her habit of relating everything temporal to the spiritual life. In her mind all of life is connected to God—even wildflowers.

So what would a wildflower talk about? Why, the greatness of God, of course! "If a wild flower could talk, I imagine it would tell us quite candidly about all God has done for it; there would be no point in hushing up his gifts to it." Thérèse greatly desires to tell anyone who will listen about her wonderful Lord and all blessings. Here she radically departs from how we would speak of the Lord. Often we hesitate to tell what the Lord has done in us for fear of sounding proud. Thérèse, on the other hand, gladly writes her story of God's blessing on her life.

Did Thérèse ever expect anyone to read this childlike record? I doubt it. Her sister Pauline obviously recognized the saintliness of the writing. But did it enter Thérèse's head that she might one day be thought a saint? Not a chance! She simply loved to praise her Lord for the wonderful life she had been blessed with—"all undeserved," she said.

That Thérèse didn't consider herself special is obvious in the next lines: "I fully realise that there was nothing about me which could have claimed [God's] divine attention; anything which is good in me is the effect of [God's] mercy—that and nothing else."

Why do we find it so hard to achieve a balance between the attitude *I am what I am by God's mercy* and false modesty? Thérèse rules out false modesty in her lines about "mock humility, and pretending that it [the little flower] was ugly, that it had no smell, that the sun had robbed it of its bloom, or the wind broken its stem, knowing that all that wasn't true."

These lines all sound reminiscent of our attempts to sound humble.

How many times have you complimented someone on a beautiful song, only to have the person say "Oh no, it wasn't any good" or "Oh no, that wasn't me; it was the Lord"? I always long to respond, "Yes, I know we are nothing without God, but I wanted to affirm you for letting God use you."

Thérèse, on the other hand, is so sure that it is *all* God that she doesn't waste words assuring others that what they see in her is not her own accomplishment. She sounds refreshingly pleased with who she is and is becoming. We sense only her joy in her Lord's favors to her and none of this mock humility. She cannot pretend she is "ugly" or has no "bloom." She is a beautiful flower—but only Jesus can make a flower, so she needn't even pretend humility. And isn't this true humility—to know that all you are has come from God?

We do not have to discount being able to sing well or any other gift God has given us. Of course we didn't give ourselves a beautiful voice! But we can choose whether to use it for God—and this is another of Thérèse's key thoughts here. Humility requires that we take whatever we have been favored with, whatever we are—and use it for the Lord. Then we may rejoice in our gifts without fear of pride. Humility remembers the source of all good gifts and still rejoices in being "gifted."

"It was he that chose the soil I was to grow in—holy ground, all steeped . . . in the scent of purity," Thérèse writes. This is perhaps one of the hardest issues in the Christian life—accepting the flower that we are.

Thérèse rejoices in the "soil" (home life) she has been given. But not everyone is planted in such rich soil. Some of us may feel like weeds planted in a vacant lot. On the other hand, some Christians do seem to have charmed lives. I am thinking of a woman I have envied. She cannot recall any negative memories in her growing-up years. She had loving Christian parents. She has been a size 12 since her early teens and is tall too. Both she and her husband have fulfilling jobs teaching at a Christian college. I imagine that she, along with Thérèse, would agree that God chose well the soil of her cultivation.

I, on the other hand, can always think of several things I would change about my soil composition, fertilizer, and climate. But I must accept the soil I was given. If I am not content with my current situation, I need at least to view it as holy ground—the place where God is with me. Holy ground is anywhere God is present. Any moment, any circumstance can become a place of blessing and holiness when I acknowledge the divine presence with me.

Jesus' presence was Thérèse's only concern. She saw her life as holy ground. No wonder she was full of joy. ❧

Reflection

1. Do you consider yourself a "little flower Jesus has picked"? Why or why not?

2. How do you respond when someone compliments you on your gifts? How easily do you accept praise, knowing that any gift you have is because of God's grace?

3. What do you find yourself telling others about most often: your miseries or God's blessings?

4. How would you describe the soil in which you've grown up?

5. Where and when did you last see your life as holy ground?

Scripture

• Exodus 3:1-14
• Philippians 2:1-18
• Matthew 13:18-23
• Matthew 13:24-30

Exercise

Spend some time remembering a "holy ground" experience in your life. If you cannot think of one, ask the Lord to show you people and places in your life where God is active but you have not recognized it as holy ground. Work at seeing God in your daily activities—recognizing those holy places and rejoicing over them.

Vow of Obedience

*A*s it is, I've ceased to be my own mistress, this long while back; I've given myself up entirely to Jesus instead, so he is at liberty to do exactly what he likes with me. He gave me this longing for complete exile, and at the same time he made it clear to me what sufferings such a life would involve; was I ready to drink the chalice of its dregs? Immediately, I put out my hand to take it, this cup Jesus was offering me; but he, thereupon, held it back, and let me see that all he wanted was my willingness to accept it.

Isn't it extraordinary, Mother, what a lot of nervous strain you can avoid by taking the vow of obedience? How enviable it is, the simple creed of the religious [one], who has only one compass to steer by, the will of her superiors! She knows for certain, all the time, that she is on the right path; there's no fear that she can go wrong, even when she feels fairly certain that her superiors are wrong.[5]

What a countercultural message Thérèse is for today! What woman in the twenty-first century would embrace the role of "ceasing to be my own mistress"? Why have we, as women, worked so hard for liberation only to give it away?

What could have possessed Thérèse to give up her freedom, even in her unliberated century? She responds in this way: "I've given myself up entirely to Jesus instead, so he is at liberty to do exactly what he likes with me." Does this sound like a woman who is worried about losing herself—or anything else? Thérèse had learned the most important lesson in the spiritual life: If you have Jesus, you have it all. *All.*

We spend so much of our prayer time asking for the things of God instead of God's self. Our God is a living being with a divine nature who longs to share with us all of that infinite divine self. We have not because we ask not. Those things that money cannot buy are available in the presence of God: serenity, perspective, forgiveness, grace. Possessing all of these graces will help us through any situation, any material need.

Thérèse also recognized that if she gave Jesus complete liberty with her life, the burdens would be pleasant ones. Her trust in Jesus was absolute. She said essentially, "He can do what he likes with me." She believed that whatever he asked of her, he would also give her the grace to bear. Do we believe this at the deepest levels of our being where life choices are transacted? If we truly trust the Jesus we profess, we can go anywhere and bear anything with serenity, perspective, and grace.

This concept convicts me at the moment as my husband and I attempt to discern a path for our future ministry. Do we trust Jesus enough to let go of all our hopes and preferences for years to come? It feels like free fall from a high altitude. Do I believe that our parachute will inflate—or will we crash? For me, the struggle is more a desire for *my* preferences than difficulty in believing that Jesus is trustworthy. I have a plan and I desperately want to work the plan. My preferences *feel* critically important, but in reality they aren't. I've lived enough years with myself and with the Lord to know that my preferences aren't always the wisest. The Lord's plan will prove to be perfect. But because I can't see the outcome, I cling to my plan, my preferences. Oh, I've prayed "not my will, but yours"—but still it's a daily battle. Thérèse had given up this battle to reside in rest.

All of the praise we can heap on Thérèse does not negate her struggles with her humanity. She questions whether she can handle the inevitable suffering. We have no hint how long she hesitated before she acquiesced to drink the dregs. How delighted the Lord must have been with her willingness! And what a pleasant surprise for Thérèse to find no suffering required of her once she was willing.

The most striking line of this passage for me is this: "Isn't it extraordinary, Mother, what a lot of nervous strain you can avoid by taking the vow of obedience?" I wonder how much of our "nervous strain" is caused by trying to force our own will on life and, more importantly, on the Lord? When I reflect on my stresses, most of them are related to getting my own way—meeting a deadline despite interruptions, avoiding some worrisome possibility, or talking God into my plan. I waste much mental energy worrying about things I cannot control—and that God seems unwilling to control.

For Thérèse the answer to this dilemma is taking a vow of obedience and trusting that the Lord is sovereign, even through the medium of her superiors. Actually, her vow of obedience only restates her trust in Christ to do what he wills with her. She will obey the Lord, whatever comes.

This affirmation rings true for me. It's quite simple: I surrender my will to the living Christ. Through this surrender I agree to trust Christ with my life and to obey him alone. Where, then, is the need for stress or strain? Life is reduced to trust. As the hymn says, "Trust and obey, for there's no other way to be happy in Jesus, but to trust and obey."[6] ❧

Reflection

1. What situation immediately comes to mind for you as a source of stress?

2. In what areas of your life have you tried to convince God to acquiesce to your preferences?

3. When have you surrendered your life to the Lord? Would you say that still holds true?

4. What does it mean for you to drink a cup of suffering? Are you willing to do so?

5. What part of today's reading grabs you? Spend some time meditating on it.

Scripture

• Psalm 119:33-40
• Deuteronomy 11:8-32
• Joshua 1:1-9
• Proverbs 3:5-6
• John 14:1-15

Exercise

In your journal, think back over your journey with God. Have you ever felt as if the Lord let you down? Recall some fears. Did the things you feared happen? Even if you answered yes, was God present in those situations with you? Reflect on the Lord's faithfulness, and consider times when you wasted energy in not believing rather than counting on God's faithfulness.

A Lover's Kiss

*W*hat comfort it brought to me, that first kiss our Lord imprinted on my soul! A lover's kiss; I knew that I was loved, and I, in my turn, told [Christ] that I loved him, and was giving myself to him for all eternity. It [has been] a long time now since he had made any demands on me; there [have] been no struggles, no sacrifices; we had exchanged looks, he and I, insignificant though I was, and we had understood one another. And now it wasn't a question of looks; something had melted away, and there were no longer two of us—Thérèse had simply disappeared, like a drop lost in the ocean; Jesus only was left, my Master, my King. Hadn't I begged him to take away my liberty, because I was so afraid of the use I might make of it; hadn't I longed, weak and helpless as I was, to be united once for all with that divine Strength?

So deep was my joy, so overpowering, that I couldn't contain myself; before long, tears of happiness were pouring down my cheeks, to the astonishment of my companions. . . . I had no room for any feeling but joy.[7]

In this reflection Thérèse recalls her first Communion at age thirteen. I am amazed that any thirteen-year-old girl could offer herself to Jesus with such conviction. I wonder exactly what Thérèse means by her reference to a "lover's kiss." In some unique way, her Lord expressed love to her. She experienced the Lord's love affectively (emotionally and physically) as a kiss. We need not dismiss her thirteen-year-old fervor as mere romanticism.

I believe the Lord would deal with us more often in affective ways if we did not rationalize away such experiences. Since the Enlightenment in the 1700s, Christians have tended to look askance at any religious experience that reason and logic cannot explain. While we must always test our experiences by scripture, don't we all crave vivid experiences of God? Don't we envy the saints for having such experiences?

The saints' dreams, visions, "words" from the Lord, and "kisses" were real to them. And while we can never enter into another person's experience, who are we to declare these experiences false? If God chose to "kiss" a thirteen-year-old French saint-in-the-making on the most important day of her young life, we should be thrilled—and perhaps envious.

Thérèse offered herself to the Lord "for all eternity." She had no doubts about whether she could remain true. She had "told [Christ] that I loved him," and that settled the matter. She considered herself married to her Lord, and her thoughts held no concept of divorce. "We had exchanged looks, he and I, . . . and we had understood one another," she writes. If you didn't know better, you could mistake this lover for a human lover. Her images are so lifelike: kisses and exchanging looks and speech.

We even hear a hint of consummation to this marriage: "There were no longer two of us." Spiritual union is a common theme among saints. Women saints often thought of the Lord as a lover or a husband and described their experiences of God in language somewhat like that in Song of Solomon. But at age thirteen, Thérèse probably would not have known enough about sex to think of her relationship with the Lord in those terms. Rather, she longed to be so close to her Lord and so united in spirit that *she* simply ceased to exist: "Thérèse had simply disappeared, like a drop lost in the ocean."

Thérèse desired to become spiritually absorbed into her Lord. This sounds strange to us, because our culture advocates exercising individual will instead of surrendering complete control of oneself to another. Thérèse reflects, "Hadn't I begged him to take away my liberty, because I was so afraid of the use I might make of it?" To her, being absorbed into Christ meant being purified. She wanted her Lover to possess complete control over her; then her entire life could be pleasing to Christ. She desired to be "united once for all with that divine Strength."

We could criticize Thérèse for looking for an easy way out of spiritual battles. Does she possibly mean that if she possessed no will but

her Lord's, she would be unable to sin? Perhaps she longed for a sure-
fire way to avoid sin's temptations. Who doesn't? I have often wished
to rise above certain sins that beset me. I remember telling my spiritual director how I could not seem to conquer an area of my life. I was
stunned and saddened to hear her reply that we can improve our weaknesses, but only heaven can purify all our infirmities. (Secretly I had
hoped to overcome this sin on my own. Alas, even my best intentions
are infiltrated with pride.)

No, Thérèse was not simply seeking to avoid temptation.
Throughout her life, she consistently strived for purity of heart and
mind and will. She longed to live a life that pleased her Lord, and she
craved signs of approval (kisses) from God.

Thérèse's line "I had no room for any feeling but joy . . ." tells us
much about her heart's desires. Her first Communion and confirma-
tion, long anticipated, represented a day when she would become one
with her Lover, the Lord. No shortcuts for her. Instead she sought
something much harder—total surrender in a manner few humans
ever accomplish.

So what application can we find in these lofty lines that sound so
foreign to our desires and experiences of God? I'm not sure we can
directly apply them to our own lives, but I do believe that if we take
the time to listen carefully, the Lord will help us discern some truths
from Thérèse's joyous memories. ❧

Reflection

1. Have you ever thought about the Lord as your lover? If not, how do you respond to this concept?

2. Have you ever experienced God's "kiss imprinted on your soul"? How did this affect you?

3. What about this passage most appeals to the desires of your heart for your own relationship with the Lord?

4. How do you respond to the idea of losing yourself "like a drop in the ocean" of God's love?

5. For what situations do you need divine strength?

Scripture

- Matthew 26:36-46
- Romans 12:1-2
- James 4:13-17
- 1 Peter 3:13-18
- Song of Solomon 1:1-4

Exercise

Renew your love vows to the Lord by reading through Song of Solomon and praying these verses to God.

Mortification

I came to realize that this respite was a precious opportunity, and decided to give myself up, more than ever, to a recollected and mortified way of life. When I say "mortified," I don't mean to suggest that I went in for penitential practices of any kind. That's a thing, I'm afraid, I've never done; I've heard so much about saintly people who took on the most rigorous mortifications from their childhood upwards, but I'd never tried to imitate them—the idea never had any attractions for me. . . . What I did try to do by way of mortification was to thwart my self-will, which always seemed determined to get its own way—to repress the rejoinder which sometimes came to my lips; to do little acts of kindness without attaching any importance to them; to sit upright instead of leaning back in my chair. That wasn't much, was it? But I did make these insignificant efforts to make myself less unworthy of a heavenly Bridegroom; and this period of apprenticeship has left tender memories behind it.[8]

Self-mortification is a foreign and undesirable concept in our culture. *Sure, we can be Christians,* we think, *but let's be comfortable, middle class, and still have things our own way.*

The Lord seems to work with me in themes. Lately the theme has been how much our culture has infected the way we view a Christian lifestyle. The killer virus of consumerism reigns. Comfort foods are featured in newspapers and Web sites. Americans, including Christians, live by the law of instant gratification, not mortification. Most of us are geared to think, *I must get what I want, and I will have it—now.*

Granted, living as addicted consumers is much easier in our era than in Thérèse's. She never suffered the temptations of fast-food restaurants and a Wal-Mart on every corner. Addictive spending was not really possible in her day. But suppose she had lived in a culture where material things were valued so much. I wonder whether Thérèse would have fallen prey to media-induced spending. Probably not, with the attitude reflected in this excerpt. Thérèse monitored her every attitude, every motivation—and measured it against her knowledge of Christ and scripture. She modeled her life on scripture, not culture.

Thérèse exhibited remarkable discipline in every area of her life. She came from an upper-middle-class family, yet she owned little. She gave up her few prized possessions to enter the convent. Taking a vow of poverty was the norm for monastic communities; the inhabitants of those communities owned nothing except their clothes. The community shared everything else—anytime a nun or monk received money, she or he gave it to the convent for the good of all.

But Thérèse went beyond material things in her vow of poverty. She determined to live in poverty of spirit, which is infinitely harder. She disciplined her tongue when instead she longed to speak. No one, no matter how saintly, avoids being irritated by others (especially when living communally).

Later in her story, Thérèse told of a nun who "has the knack of rubbing me up the wrong way at every turn; her tricks of manner, her tricks of speech, her character, just strike me as unlovable." So what did she do? She practiced holding her tongue when she really desired to correct or rebuke this woman. Also, she recalled that God must love this woman dearly, so "I determined to treat this sister as if she were the person I loved best in the world."

Incredibly, this sister came to Thérèse at one point and said, "I wish you would tell me . . . what it is about me that gets the right side of you? You've always got a smile for me whenever I see you." Thérèse remarked in her autobiography that what really attracted her about the woman was "Jesus hidden in the depths of her soul."[9] Obviously Thérèse succeeded in her quest to overcome both her tongue and her attitude toward this "unlovable" woman.

Thérèse described the purpose of her goal of mortification as being to "thwart my self-will, which always seemed determined to get its own way." How does anyone gain mastery over self-will? I confess that my efforts have been pitifully unsuccessful. I determine that I will not criticize—and then almost as soon as the words are out of my mouth, I catch myself doing just that. Or I decide that I will not complain (another means of demanding my own way), but I fail miserably. Oh, I have my justification: I am an idealist, and I want so much from this life! What I really want is things my way. Why can't others see things my way—the right way? One way I attempt to correct myself is to remind myself: *The world does not need my opinion.* So in committees or at home I try not to say what *I* want or like. It's a constant struggle; I'm sure Thérèse would concur.

Thérèse also fought her battle by trying "to do little acts of kindness without attaching any importance to them." I assume she means to do acts of kindness without advertising it or making the recipients of these acts feel that they owe her favors. I too try to practice random acts of kindness. The hard part is not telling anyone! When we actually manage a selfless act, then we ruin it by broadcasting it proudly.

Every saint, it seems, had unique and quirky habits of mortification. What good is gained from sitting up straight in your chair instead of leaning back? How is God's kingdom benefited by this inconsequential act? Quite indirectly. Thérèse becomes a more disciplined person. This discipline spills over into other areas of her life, which affects her fellow nuns, and they, in turn, become better nuns. Doing good is always contagious. And even if it only made her feel virtuous, that was her goal, and a good one.

Sister Colette, my spiritual director in Rochester, once said to me, "Discipline is remembering what you *really* want." Thérèse never forgot what she really wanted. She constantly disciplined herself with small mortifications. May we go and do likewise. ✺

Reflection

1. What is your initial response to the idea of self-mortification as self-discipline? Why?

2. What ways have you practiced denying yourself in order to become more Christlike?

3. In what ways has Thérèse inspired you to try again? What habits do you need to denounce? What habits do you want to establish?

4. What disciplines of speech do you need to begin?

5. What unseen, kind act can you do today for someone—and keep it a secret?

Scripture

- Matthew 23:25-26
- 2 Timothy 3:1-5
- Ephesians 2:1-5
- Hebrews 12:5-13

Exercise

Spend some time journaling about your self-will. First, trying drawing it. What image comes to mind? Meditate on this image. What scripture passage comes to mind? Read the passage and ask God to open the passage to you with new insight. Then ask the Lord to help you with self-renunciation.

Dark Night

*B*ut no, it was night everywhere, a deep night enfolding my soul; I felt, like our Lord in his Agony, that I was quite alone, without anything in heaven or on earth to console me; God himself seemed to have abandoned me. All those three days nature itself seemed to be in tune with my state of mind; there was never a ray of sunshine, and the rain fell in torrents. At all the critical moments of my life, I've found that nature seemed to be the mirror of my own soul's condition.[10]

I ought really to have said something about the retreat I made before my profession. It brought no consolation with it, only complete dryness and almost a sense of dereliction. Once more, our Lord was asleep on the boat.[11]

All the great saints write about their "dark night" experiences. Saint John of the Cross wrote an entire book called *The Dark Night of the Soul.* What happens in a "dark night"? Not much. God seems absent and prayers empty.

In this excerpt Thérèse recounts such a time as she neared her entry date to Carmel Convent. With her long-awaited entrance to the convent drawing near, one would expect her to be ecstatic, spiritually and emotionally. She made a retreat to pray and prepare herself with this great goal's end in view. What was her experience? A dark night of spiritual emptiness and prayers as dry as dust.

Saint Ignatius called it "desolation" of soul and heart. Perhaps the dark night is caused by some grievous circumstance, or there appears to be no cause. Cause is irrelevant while we're consumed with the feeling that we have fallen into the abyss. The reason we feel this way is because we sense that God is no longer with us. Oh, how much we depend on feeling good about our times with God!

Bruce Demarest, in his book *Satisfy Your Soul*, says of the dark night:

> Spiritually God's absence creates a vacuum that can show us the emptiness
> of our fleshly attachments, such as our dependence on people and things for
> a security they cannot give. . . . When we let go of these attachments, then
> we are propelled toward Christlikeness.[12]

When I read this quote recently, suddenly I found an explanation for a long, dark night in my soul in 1999. The word *vacuum* held the key to my insight. I had clung tenaciously to my ideal job/home/family dream. But when God's presence evaporated and aridity lasted for months, I cared not for my beloved plan but gasped only my Beloved's name. Life had truly become a vacuum that none of my plans could fill. God's absence weaned me of several worldly attachments. What good are things without the joy of the Lord?

Thérèse's words about a "deep night enfolding my soul" sound all too familiar. She (and I) felt quite alone. "God . . . seemed to have abandoned me." Even when we know that the dark night will end, we still shudder at the thoughts of how long the night can seem. Thérèse must have been very disappointed to experience a dark night just before her entry into Carmel, when otherwise she would have been so excited.

Amazingly, "complete dryness" and "deep night" are God's ways of refining us. We cannot fathom what refining the Lord meant to accomplish in Thérèse before she could enter the convent. As for my "dark night" experience, I see now that God desired me to turn loose of many of my cherished plans. Not only did I think I knew best, but I was also trying to tell God how to manage my life. Paradoxically, darkness enlightened me; I finally realized that without God my idyll is hell, not heaven.

How do we get through a dark night of the soul? We learn to walk in the dark. We keep on praying despite the dryness. We continue believing despite God's silence and seeming absence. Thérèse's mental picture of the Lord's being asleep on the boat helped her persevere. This image implies God's presence but withdrawal as well.

We need to remember that God does not withdraw because of anger at us. Rather, the Lord trusts us to steer the boat alone for a short while.

Even though I hate dark spiritual times, I have learned to hold fast during them, knowing that one morning I will awaken, and the dry spell will have mysteriously ended. God is done with refining me for the time being, and I feel like a prisoner set free.

I was helped tremendously when I realized that "dark night" times are normal in spiritual development. I spent months of my first "dark night" experience agonizing over what I must have done to cause God to withdraw.

During such times discussing your desolation with a spiritual guide can help you gain perspective. God may seem to have abandoned us, but we must remember that the feeling is only temporary. After all, God's Word reminds us time and again that God is faithful and that God will never abandon us. ✌

Reflection

1. Have you ever experienced a "dark night" in your spiritual development? If so, how did you respond?

2. What good feelings do you rely on in your quiet times?

3. When have you felt as if God had abandoned you?

4. What is your prayer life like at the moment?

5. How is spiritual dryness manifested in your prayer life?

Scripture

- John 14:15-31
- Joshua 1:1-5
- Acts 1:1-11
- Luke 24:13-35
- 1 Kings 19:1-13

Exercise

Choose one of the above passages and meditate on the presence of the Lord and the promise that God will never abandon us. Then try to look at your own dryness in light of these promises.

*F*or some time past, I had indulged the fancy of offering myself up to the Child Jesus as a plaything, for him to do what he liked with me. I don't mean an expensive plaything; give a child an expensive toy, and he will sit looking at it without daring to touch it. But a toy of no value—a ball, say—is all at his disposal: he can throw it on the ground, kick it about, make a hole in it, leave it lying in a corner, or press it to his heart if he feels that way about it. In the same way, I wanted our Lord to do exactly what he liked with me: and here, in Rome, he'd taken me at my word. . . . Well, suppose the child makes a hole in the ball to see what's inside it, and then, satisfied with that, throws the ball away and goes to sleep. Who's to tell us what the child's dreaming about, while the ball lies there neglected? Perhaps he dreams that he's still playing with it, first dropping it and then picking it up, letting it roll a long way away and then pressing it to his heart, to make sure that it never slips from his hand again. Yes, he can do just what he likes; but you see, Mother, it's a depressing sensation to feel you're like the ball that's been thrown on one side.[13]

This excerpt doesn't sound like Thérèse unless you understand the context. At Thérèse's urging, her father had taken her to Rome to beseech the pope for a special dispensation for Thérèse to enter the convent at age fifteen. The pope received her warmly and listened politely, but replied that if God meant for her to enter the convent early, she would. He sent her back to her local bishop, allowing him to decide. It sounds as if the pope dismissed a schoolgirl's idealistic wish, but he didn't know her and probably chose the wisest path, considering that she might have been completely unfit for the convent.

Thérèse, however, whose dearest wish had been denied, took this decision very hard, prompting her mature reflection above. She received her larger wish—that God might be free to do with her as God wished. (She did receive permission to enter the convent within a few months, but today's reading records her immediate response to the pope's decision.)

Thérèse exhibited a wonderful sense of childlikeness in her writing, never more delightfully than in this excerpt. She viewed herself as a toy ball, inexpensive and ordinary—the kind a child would favor but no adult would understand why. She imaginatively envisioned herself as a toy ball for the child Jesus. Scripture gives us so little information about Christ's childhood that few of us ever imagine Jesus as a regular boy—playing ball, for instance.

Yet scripture tells us that Jesus was fully human. Most of us don't deal well with the humanity of Jesus, though; we shy away from it. What would an eight-year-old Jesus be like? How different would he be from any eight-year-old boy? Was he full of mischief? Did he play hard and get dirty? If we are to believe scripture, he lived and played like any boy. Thérèse obviously thought so. She imagines him playing ball—but with her as the ball!

Now, anyone who knows boys and balls knows that you don't have to tell them how to play with the ball. They just do whatever comes naturally—sometimes throwing it as hard as their young muscles allow, sometimes just carrying it everywhere they go. Although Thérèse had no biological brothers, she knew about boys and balls. She even knew that sometimes they make holes in a ball just to see what it's made of, and she freely imagined herself as the object of the child Jesus' boyish whims. What abandon Thérèse exhibited in offering herself to Jesus! She wrote, "I had indulged the fancy of offering myself up to the Child Jesus as a plaything, for him to do what he liked with me."

I would like to ask Thérèse, "How can you be so unconcerned about your life?" If she lived in our culture, we would probably say to her, "Get a life, Thérèse!" Our culture operates on the premise that *we* choose what we will do, then we ask God to bless it. (We may never confess that we operate out of this premise, but we do so nonetheless.) Thérèse, in contrast, didn't have a care in the world about her life's outcome. Jesus could do what he liked with her—even poke a hole in her or leave her forgotten in a corner.

I confess that I am full of opinions about my future. Wisely, I plan my daily life and my future vocation, goals, and outcomes (like a good lesson plan). Somewhere along my spiritual journey, I surrendered my life outcomes to the Lord, only to discover that I still have more opinions to surrender. But my greatest discovery was that *I* had planned how I would grow spiritually without consulting the Spirit at all. My desire to grow spiritually consumes me, but somehow I wrongly assumed that I would be responsible for my own growth. Then I had to surrender those plans as well.

Thérèse knew no such battles. She knew from her earliest years that she belonged to the child Jesus and that he alone would arrange her life. Certainly she's despondent at this point in her desire to enter the convent early. But she knew it was only a matter of her impatience. She was certain that the child Jesus loved her and that he would pick her up again and again, as if she were a favorite toy. ❧

Reflection

1. Have you ever thought about what Jesus was like as a child? Is his childhood real to you? Why or why not?

2. Could you give yourself to Jesus as a toy to be played with or ignored?

3. How would you respond if Jesus left you lying in the corner of his room—if he didn't choose to use you for his kingdom for a while?

4. In what ways have you surrendered the outcome of your life to the Lord?

Scripture

- Luke 2:41-52
- Psalm 51:15-17
- Matthew 10:37-39
- Matthew 6:25-33

Exercise

Imagine yourself as a ball in the hands of the child Jesus. Allow him to treat you as he wants. Spend a few minutes vividly picturing Jesus as a boy and yourself as the ball in his young hands. Afterward, reflect: How did you feel about entrusting yourself to this child Jesus?

Artist and Canvas

*I*f the canvas on which an artist is working could think and speak, it obviously wouldn't be annoyed with the brush that kept on touching and retouching it; and it wouldn't be envious either, because it would know perfectly well that all its beauty came from the artist who held the brush, not from the brush itself. And on the other side, the brush couldn't claim any credit for the masterpiece on which it was at work, because it would know quite well that artists are never at a loss; they are the sort of people who enjoy coming up against difficulties, and find it amusing, sometimes, to make use of shoddy and imperfect instruments.

Well, dear Mother, I'm the poor little brush our Lord has picked out to be the means of imprinting his image on the souls which you have entrusted to me.... I'm the little tiny brush which he uses afterwards, to put in the extra flourishes.[14]

Thérèse exhibits the most natural humility of any author I've ever read. Hers isn't a false humility or a devaluing of her gifts. She recognizes that without God she is insignificant, a blank canvas.

Thérèse delightfully uses the analogy of an artist painting on a blank canvas. We are the canvas, and our Lord is the artist painting divine beauty onto the canvas of our lives. She also speaks of brush techniques—how the artist keeps retouching the painting. How similar this analogy is to our spiritual lives! God indeed paints a picture of the divine image on our lives, and the Master Artist must do many retouchings, since we often try to be the artist rather than the canvas, and we keep messing up the picture.

Thérèse reminds us that the canvas knows that the brush is not the source of beauty. Instead, the artist handling the brush determines the shades and outlines of the masterpiece in his or her imagination. God looks at me and envisions what I will look like someday when the Master Artist places the finishing touches on my canvas. Each person is a work of art. But how easy it is to forget that we are not the artist. How often we pull out our own paint tubes and mix gaudy colors, smearing them and obliterating the Artist's design. So how do we learn to let God be the artist and accept the design God is painting onto our lives?

First, we need to be sensitive to recurring themes in our lives. As I've said previously, God often works in themes in my life. For weeks or months at a time, I will notice the same idea or theme appearing in the books I read, sermons I hear, or thoughts that come to me in prayer. I believe these are brush strokes God is painting into my character, enriching my beauty. Currently the theme is the value of relationships and community. For many months grace was a theme for me—one I needed to incorporate into my spiritual life.

Another way to determine God's artistic hand at work on us is by discerning the meaning in hard times. When I go through a particularly bad patch, I redouble my efforts to understand what lesson I am supposed to learn from it. The darker areas of my painting usually appear during trials. If I can hear God's words to me during that time, it helps me bear with the painful brush strokes. If I could, I would choose all colorful, vivid experiences in my spiritual life and avoid the dark times. But any artist will tell you that the darker colors are what make the vivid hues stand out.

Still another way to interpret the Artist's design is through scripture. What scriptures do you feel drawn to? The Psalms appeal to many people, especially during emotional times. The Book of Job offers comfort in suffering. The Pentateuch (first five books of the Old Testament) speaks to us of God's power. And the Gospels generally enrich our intimacy with Jesus. Those areas of scripture to which we feel drawn give us clues for what the Artist may be sketching in our lives. We can cooperate with the Master's artistic hand by pondering the scriptures and applying them to our current life situations.

Occasionally we may find the Artist painting something completely surprising onto our life's canvas. Suddenly a new vocation opens up before us, or a new character is painted onto the scene. God is infinitely creative and often unpredictable. Let the Master paint in some surprises.

Thérèse calls herself the "little tiny brush" the artist uses to put in the last touches. We are both the canvas and the brushes of God—instruments to share the Artist's design with the world. We cannot claim the design as our own, nor the paint nor the mastery. We are merely brushes that God uses—and paradoxically, we are the canvas at the same time.

Thérèse understands that it's all about God, the artist—not about her, the instrument. God is the artist; she is simply an insignificant brush or canvas.

Brush and canvas—but never the artist—that is our relationship with the Lord, the Artist of the universe. We are here to wear God's beauty on the canvas of our lives and to act as brushes, painting flourishes when and where God wills. ✑

Reflection

1. What colors is God painting into your life at the moment? What sort of theme characterizes your life?

2. How much can you see of God's design for your life?

3. How and where is God using you to paint flourishes?

4. How easy is it for you to give up control of the design and let the Lord paint your life?

Scripture

- Genesis 1
- Job 38
- Psalm 8
- Revelation 21
- Psalm 139

Exercise

Sit prayerfully, imagining what God is painting in your life now. Then draw whatever picture comes to mind. Try to see what God is doing with you and through you in this depiction of the Artist's image in your life. Or leaf through a book of masterpieces and try to imagine what scenes and colors God is using to paint you.

I may never have full rest nor

very bliss ... until I become

so fastened to God

that there is nothing

between my God and me.

—Julian of Norwich

Meet Julian of Norwich

What an interesting viewpoint we get when all we know of someone is what we find in that person's writing. Julian comes close to fitting this description. Little is known of her personal life—but, oh, what an impact her writing makes.

Why has Julian's writing been so influential? Was it because she was the first woman to write a literary work in English? Was it due to the extraordinary visions she received from God? Or perhaps because her rich descriptions of God's love can't help but make an impact on us? The answer to all these questions is yes.

However, Julian could well represent women of our time, with her understanding of the mothering/nurturing characteristics of God. Who but God could have given her this insight? Certainly not the culture of her day.

What do we know about Julian? She lived in England, was born around 1342, and was still alive in 1413 (our last dated reference). But no one is sure where she was born or how long she lived. She may have come from a wealthy family, since she was educated, and few females in that day were offered that opportunity. She probably studied in a convent, probably Benedictine, perhaps near Norwich.

Her real name probably wasn't even Julian, since most nuns took on a saint's name. Julian happened to live in the Saint Julian Church in Norwich, hence her name. Julian was an anchorite. Anchorites took vows of isolation to devote themselves to prayer. They lived in cells on the outside wall of the church. Each cell had a window looking into the church (to enable the anchorites to participate in church services) and a window facing out to the world. Literally, the windows of the anchorites' cells opened onto the main street of the town, enabling anyone desiring spiritual guidance to speak to the anchorites in their cells. Julian spent her time praying and offering spiritual direction through her outer window.

Interestingly, a woman named Margery Kempe documented Julian's spiritual direction ministry in a book. Margery was the first woman to write an autobiography in English, and she mentions the benefit of discussing spiritual matters with Julian. (See *The Book of Margery Kempe* in "Suggested Reading.")

The Middle Ages are one of my favorite eras of history, but I would not have wanted to live during this period. It was a time of political unrest between France and England, as well as distress and corruption in the Catholic Church in Rome. The goal of most people was merely to stay alive. Bubonic plague, an epidemic that ravaged Europe between 1347 and 1351, is estimated to have killed as much as one-third of Europe's population in some places. Living in her isolated cell during this time might have been an important factor in Julian's survival amidst the "Black Death." She must have been touched by the immense suffering in her world.

So what message does Julian have for us today? After reading *Revelations of Divine Love* (also known as *Showings*), I am tempted to write this entire book on Julian's insights alone. But I will focus on two: her emphasis on God's immense love for each of us, and her insight into the motherlike characteristics of God. Both are deep needs for me—to know I am deeply loved by God and that God longs to tenderly nurture my femininity. I suspect that these needs are universal for women. Julian thought so, and thus her writing is relevant to us 650 years later.

Today's women often feel fragmented, trying to do many things, with the result that they feel they are doing nothing well. I think that Julian would respond to this frustration and stress by saying, "Let God love you and 'all shall be well.'"

This is also my hope as you ponder her "showings" from God. God has not changed, and God's words to Julian still hold truth for us. I have paraphrased her words into more familiar language. Ponder the wisdom and apply it to your hearts. Let God tenderly love you through Julian's words.

Maker, Keeper, Lover

*G*od showed me a hazelnut, in the palm of my hand, and it was as round as a ball. . . .

In this little thing I saw three characteristics. The first is that God made it, the second is that God loves it, and the third, that God "keeps" it [cares for it]. But what does this mean to me, that God is Maker, Keeper, Lover? Until I am oned [united] with God, I will never understand the bliss of God as my maker or keeper or lover. Or to say it another way, I want to be so united with God that there is nothing between my God and me.[1]

We might easily discount Julian's passion for God by saying she didn't have a family, a job—in short, a life—so it must have been easy for her to think about spiritual things. She didn't try to maintain a house, a career, and a daily planner. So do we write her off as irrelevant? Only at our souls' peril.

How, then, does a hazelnut relate to our lives? The hazelnut symbolizes something small and insignificant. Julian implies that each of us is small and insignificant in God's great, cosmic plan—yet God loves this little, ordinary nut. Julian gently reminds us that if God fashioned every tiny element of creation, then that same care (and more!) was lavished on creating you and me.

Since God created us, we have no right to question why a nose is too long or hips are too wide. Our Maker had a design for us—the best possible design for our lives. Raving at God over a bodily characteristic that cannot be changed is wasted time (no matter what our society says). We are creatures, not creators. Our Maker has lovingly fashioned us. Even more important, we bear the image of God stamped in each of us—the "designer label" each of us should proudly wear. And the only appropriate response to our Maker is to bow in worship.

How does God "keep" a hazelnut? I expect it's simply a matter of life cycle. But think how glorious the life cycle of a nut is. A hazel tree matures and reproduces nuts, and they fall to the ground. But does the hazelnut die? No, it falls into the soil, sprouts, and resurrects as a new tree! Could Julian mean that God carefully watches over our life cycle and oversees our transformation into a resurrected life? Yes!

We normally think of God as "Keeper" in terms of providence. We think (rightly so) that God will watch over us, protect us, and provide for our physical and material needs. But God's plan is so much larger than we imagine. God desires to keep us even into eternity! We give eternity little daily thought—and yet it is the goal of our lives. This life is not the end but a means to an end—our being made holy.

Okay, we can theologically accept Maker and Keeper, but should we think of God as Lover? Absolutely! God *is* Love. Perhaps we've heard this phrase all our lives, but we've never considered God as Lover, as Julian portrays.

Granted, Julian didn't have a husband. Paul admitted that it is easier to be single-mindedly focused on God if one doesn't marry. However, we can't dismiss Julian's passionate love relationship with God that easily. She experiences God as Lover. She states a desire to be "oned" with God—"oned" as in "the two become one." She longs to give herself completely to this Lover-God and to be absorbed in this relationship until there is no more Julian but only God.

Julian goes on to say, "I may never have full rest nor very bliss" until there is nothing between her and her Lover. But Julian spent no time questioning God as we do. We ask: "God, why did you do this? Why didn't you answer my prayer the way I wanted?"

Julian knew that she was that insignificant hazelnut in the hand of the Maker, who is also Keeper and Lover. What could she possibly say but:

- Make me what you wish;

- Keep me all the way into eternity;

- Love me till I have lost all desire except for You.

We could do much worse than to consider ourselves something small, held by a Creator who loves us and keeps us even into eternity. ✍

Reflection

1. How do you experience God as your Maker, and what effect does this have on you?

2. How is the Lord your Keeper?

3. How do you experience God as Lover?

4. How would being "oned" with God change things in your life?

5. What hinders your being "oned" with God?

Scripture

- Psalm 139
- Jeremiah 18:1-10
- Hosea 11
- Jeremiah 31:3-4

Exercise

Choose a day when you will have a more relaxed schedule than usual. Try to live that day single-mindedly focusing on God. Whenever you realize you've lost focus, begin again to dedicate your activities and mental energies to your Lover God.

Love Was the Meaning

I often desired to learn what was our Lord's meaning [regarding our relationship with God]. And fifteen years after [I began this book], I was given an insight. The Lord said: "Do you want to understand your Lord's meaning in this? Learn it well: Love was my meaning. Who showed it to you? Love. What did your Lord show you? Love. Why did your Lord show you? For love. Hold on to me and I will show you more. But you will never learn it all." Thus I understood: Love was our Lord's meaning.

And I fully understood that before God made us, God loved us; and that love has never lessened, nor ever shall. And in this love God has done all works; and in this love God made all things profitable to us; and in this love our life is everlasting. We were created out of this love which was in God since the beginning. And in this love is our beginning. And through this love is how we shall see God forever.[2]

I am often struck by how slowly God works. We know that a thousand years are like a day in God's sight—which is to say God lives outside the boundaries of time. But still it seems to take the Lord so long to answer our anxious questions. So we are the ones who must adjust to God's timing. But spending fifteen years waiting for an answer? No wonder Julian is considered a saint! For fifteen years she had prayed to understand the meaning of God's relationship with her—and when the answer came, it was so obvious. She had known it all along.

Of course love was God's meaning. God *is* love. What else could God's meaning have been? Love was and is the Lord's purpose in all of creation. We know all the right things to say about God's loving us, and love was the meaning in everything concerning us. But what about:

- a miscarriage? Where is the love meaning then?
- divorce? What does love mean to us then?
- cancer? How do we see God's love then?

We *know* that God loves us—and that our lives are

undergirded by that love. But what we know and what we feel can be galaxies apart. What happens on those days when we can't feel what we know to be true? How do we access the love of God in affective (emotional) ways?

Julian reminds us that the very air we breathe is love-soaked. The Lord says to her: "Learn it well—Love was [my] meaning."

Love showed her the meaning.

Love was all there was to show her.

Love was God's motivation for answering her.

This begins to sound quite repetitious, but love is precisely the point. The answer to the meaning of our existence is simply love. God loves us—that is the central fact of our existence and the explanation for everything God does. Life may throw at us situations like a miscarriage or divorce or cancer, but none of these situations—*nothing*—can separate us from the love of God in Christ Jesus. God's gracious love is unchanging. It has always been there and always will be.

So how do we reconcile God's all-pervasive love with life's tragedies? We must expand our image and understanding of God. Not long ago on TV, I heard a woman explain the death of her sister in a mass shooting by saying: "God must have wanted her." I longed to call this woman and tell her that God had nothing to do with a deranged man's shooting spree. Who could love such a God? Or who would believe that God loved someone so much that the Almighty sent a deranged killer to take that woman's life so that she could be in heaven with God? No. This action is not of God, nor is it of love. We must carefully separate God's actions from those of sinful humans.

The question we must learn to ask is: Where is God in all of this? Where is God's love in the midst of cancer or divorce or shootings? If God's love is the air we breathe, then that love is present in my situation, no matter how bad it seems. We must learn to look for the meaning—for God's love—as long as Julian did or however long it takes.

Love was God's meaning. Is it also ours? ⁊

Reflection

1. What question have you been asking God for a long time?

2. What answers have you discerned so far? What meaning do you see in your painful situation?

3. How do you sense God's love undergirding you in this situation?

4. How could God's love be the meaning woven into your circumstances?

5. What helps you to feel/experience God's love for you?

Scripture

• Jeremiah 31:3
• 1 Corinthians 13:7-8
• Genesis 50:20

Exercise

Recall a time when you felt God's love in a soul-satisfying way. What were the circumstances? How did you receive it? What was that like? How did it transform you?

*A*nd after this God showed a sovereign pleasure in my soul. I was filled with an everlasting sureness; all was pleasure without any painful dread. This feeling was so glad and ethereal that I was completely peaceful, and nothing on earth could have grieved me.

This lasted for a while and then it changed, and all was heaviness and weariness of life and irritation with myself so that I could hardly be bothered to live. There was no comfort nor ease. Faith, hope and charity I had in reality, but without feeling them.

And awhile after this our blessed Lord gave me again the comfort and rest of soul, so satisfying and blissful that no sorrow or pain or dread could have distressed me. And then I felt pain again; and joy and pleasure; now one and then the other for maybe twenty times. When I felt joyful, I might have said with Saint Paul: "Nothing shall separate me from the love of Christ"; and in the pain I might have said with Peter: "Lord, save me. I perish!"

The vision as I understood it then is this: It speeds spiritual growth to sometimes be comforted, and other times to feel we are left alone (by God). But God wants us to know that we are kept secure whether in comfort or in sorrow. And it is a profit to our souls to remember this: that feelings of God's absence do not mean we have sinned. There are times when God chooses not to give us "blessed" feelings. But freely our Lord gives when he will and allows us to be in sorrow sometimes. Both are God's love.[3]

As I write this, I "feel" as though God is absent. I am in a place of pain, and I want God to make it all feel better. Why doesn't God come to us with warm, comforting feelings when we think we'll die without them?

C. S. Lewis said during his grief (after his wife died) that it felt as if the door of heaven had been slammed in his face. He sensed only silence when he desperately needed to hear God's comforting voice. Lewis asked, "Where is God?"[4] That's a good question that many people have unsuccessfully tried to answer.

I don't have answers either. My guess is that in our pain God trusts us to remember that divine love is always there for us. And yes, I'd rather *feel* loved and comforted than just to remember this truth. But would feeling it make it any truer? No. I would just feel better.

Humans are such feelings-oriented creatures, but feelings are fleeting. We can feel twenty different feelings in an hour on any given day. For example, yesterday was not a "good feeling" day for me. I was on the verge of tears all day. Yet, as I walked across campus, I saw a rose blooming (in November!) and stopped to smell and gaze on this November miracle. And for just a brief moment, I knew bliss—in the midst of my pain.

Then I looked up at a gorgeous blue sky and remembered that the beauty of pink roses and blue skies originates in the love of God. In my pain, I felt bliss—and in that bliss, I knew again God's love for me. It still didn't make me feel goose bumps. No, this knowledge was better. Mere feeling was transcended by touching a deeper truth: God loves us through pain and joy and apathy. How I feel cannot change that divine love for me. The comfort, then, is to remind myself of this unchanging love when my feelings would betray God's truth.

Julian tells us a great truth in this passage: "Both are love." Feelings of comfort and feelings of God's absence are only feelings. God's love is true and everlasting no matter how I feel.

Why is it so easy to feel loved by God when all seems blessed and happy? Julian says that in her times of joy, she could shout with Saint Paul, "Nothing shall dispart [separate] me from the charity of Christ." But, it seems to me, there is one thing that can: our feelings. I can actually allow my feelings to distance me from God. What I choose to tell myself about God when I am in pain determines whether I am moving toward God's love or away from it. So Julian implores us to remember that all feelings are encompassed in love.

When God feels near, revel in the intimacy. When God feels absent, wait for the return of "good feelings." But never doubt that God's love surrounds us, nearer than we can imagine. ✍

Reflection

1. What triggers feelings of despair, pain, or depression for you?

2. What do you tell yourself about God when these feelings strike?

3. Reflect on a time you felt God's nearness. Where were you? What were you doing? What was it like? How did you respond to God?

4. Reflect on a time when you felt God's absence. What was that like? How did you respond? What did you tell yourself about waiting it out?

Scripture

- Psalms 42–43
- Psalm 46
- Psalm 73
- Psalm 91
- Psalm 103
- Psalm 131

Exercise

Sit down some evening and list the feelings you experienced that day. Think through the day's events: How did you feel in each situation? Look at how many feelings you experienced in just one day. What does that reveal about your relationship with God and the part feelings play? Record these insights in your journal for future reference.

Bliss

---

*B*ut I saw our Lord as a lord in his own house, where He called all His dear and worthy servants and friends to a stately feast. Then I saw the Lord royally reign in His house, filling it with joy and mirth endlessly to gladden and to solace His dear and worthy friends. Christ was both homely [hospitable] and courteous with a marvelous melody of endless love in His own fair blessed countenance. . . .

God showed three degrees of bliss that every soul shall have in Heaven if this soul willingly served God in any degree on earth. The first is the worshipful thanks of our Lord God that the soul shall give when it is delivered of pain. . . . The second is that all the blessed creatures that are in Heaven shall see that worshipful thanking. . . . The third is, that as new and as gladdening as it [worship] is received in that time, rightly so shall it last without end. . . .

. . . Every person shall be made known in Heaven and shall be rewarded for willing service [to God].[5]

In this reading Julian envisions a party in heaven at Christ's house. Can you picture your Lord meeting you at the door, with sounds of love and laughter in the background? Listen to the happy voices, carefree at last, rejoicing in just being together. Then remember why you are here—to receive a reward for your service to God on earth.

Step into the house, Christ's house of joy and mirth. Laugh with your friends there and let Christ gladden and console your heart, now that your trials on earth are done.

Look into your Lord's face. What do you see? Julian pictured Christ's face as full of love—smiling, laughing even, for the joy of being there together forever!

Religious art does not often depict a laughing Christ, nor do we hear about this in Sunday school. How hard is it for you to picture Christ with a sense of humor? I can think of several places in scripture where it seems to me that God chuckles. Doesn't the God who could make an orangutan have a sense of humor? Or consider Jesus' statement in Matthew 19:24 that it's easier for a camel to fit through the eye of a needle than for a rich person to enter the kingdom of heaven. Anyway, why shouldn't Christ and all of us laugh in heaven? This picture of Julian's seems bliss indeed.

Who will be invited to this party at Jesus' house? Who is being rewarded? Those who have willingly served God here on earth. I don't know what will qualify as service—nor where the line falls between willing and dutiful. But our service to God does not go unnoticed, nor, according to Revelation, does it go unrewarded. Read again about the marriage supper of the Lamb (Rev. 19:5-9). It sounds much like this passage of Julian's—a celebration for those who have served the Lamb of God.

Julian goes on to say in this chapter that all our sufferings in service to Christ will be eclipsed by the joy we will know then. She even suggests that this should be our motivation for serving. Whatever we give up now, whatever the cost of serving Christ, the reward will be greater than we can imagine.

Isn't Jesus our model for service? "Looking to Jesus the pioneer and perfecter of our faith, who for the sake of the joy that was set before him endured the cross, disregarding its shame, and has taken his seat at the right hand of the throne of God" (Heb. 12:2). Surely the throne is in the center of the celebrations!

So how should we serve? We serve in whatever way everyday life presents to us. Perhaps we baby-sit for a neighbor while she goes to the doctor, or help an elderly lady unload her groceries. Maybe we sit up at night with a sick child, or we teach a Sunday school class of sixth-grade boys.

While teaching a Sunday school class fifteen years ago, I realized that the verse about laying up treasure in heaven could mean only one thing. The only treasure we can lay up in heaven is what we have done for others. Service, then, is simply being there for others and doing whatever Christ would do for them.

Some of us serve regularly, according to our spiritual gifts. We pastor or teach or give according to our gifts and talents. But Julian (and scripture) imply that every small thing we do is noticed and recorded for that future reward in heaven. We can bring bliss to others, and yes, even to ourselves, through our service in this life—and we get invited to the rewards party at Jesus' house! ❧

Reflection

1. Do I look at service as something I *ought* to do, or do I willingly serve Christ with my gifts and my time?

2. What do I have to offer in service to God?

3. How can I make better use of my spiritual gifts to serve others?

4. What ideas for service have been lurking in the back of my mind—ways I could be serving that I haven't yet pursued?

5. What needs have I noticed around me that go unmet? How could I attempt to meet these needs?

6. What rationalizations might I offer for my unwillingness to serve God?

Scripture

- Revelation 19:5-9
- Hebrews 12:1-3
- Hebrews 13:1-3
- Romans 12

Exercise

What need could you meet for someone today? Attempt to serve someone today and keep it a secret.

Peace

*B*ut our courteous Lord wills not that His servants despair. We should not despair of ourselves when we fall often or grievously, for our falling [failing] does not hinder His love for us. Peace and love are ever in us, being and working, but we do not always let peace and love work their way in us. Our Lord wants us to take heed and remember that He is the ground of our whole life in love. [God] is our everlasting Keeper and mightily defends us against our enemies. For we give [God] occasion [to keep and defend us] by our falling.[6]

To me, the worst feeling is that of being trapped. When I am stuck in a situation that I long to escape, I struggle. I have created some of my own traps—I took on certain projects without consulting the Lord and then regretted them later. I remember starting a Bible study once (my idea) and then being totally frustrated because no one had even read, let alone studied, the scripture before meetings. The participants asked me to treat them like one of my college classes, but then they whined—and I wanted out! I felt trapped, and it was my own fault.

Other times we are trapped by our own failings, such as weight we can't lose or relationships we can't resolve, and we despair. We fall. Sometimes it is simply our humanness that traps us and causes us to fall. We long for victory over personal failings; we long to be more; and when we are not, we despair.

In such times we can read Julian's words again: "But our courteous Lord wills not that His servants despair." Evidently despair doesn't please God. Why wouldn't it? Because despair is hopelessness. The cause for that hopelessness is realizing that we cannot do something ourselves.

The wonderful truth we have so much trouble believing is that we don't have to do it by ourselves! God wants to be involved in our lives, helping us and doing it for us.

Further, we should not despair because Christ has provided peace and love to reside in us and counteract despair when we do fall (fail). He doesn't love us any less when we fail. God already knows all our weaknesses and infirmities—and expects us to fail! So the Creator has already wired into our psyches divine love and peace to help us deal with our human frailties—a spiritual immune system that fights off despair.

One of my favorite quotations about seeking God's love is from Augustine: "Thou wert within; and I without."[7] In other words, God was living inside Augustine, but he was looking outside himself to find meaning. Don't we do the same? God has provided all the resources we could ever need. Yet when we sight an "enemy," we rush headlong to fix it ourselves. When we can't, we despair. Then we wonder where God has been during this process. The Great Provider has been waiting quietly within us, waiting until we are finally willing to turn toward the source of peace and love.

What personal "enemies" ambush you? What needs or situations cause you to rush to your own defense without consulting God? My husband and I have been in a career transition for four years since returning to the States from a missions assignment. Finding a new career path has been our "enemy." Sure, we prayed, but jobs don't just drop into our laps, do they? We have to sell ourselves, put in applications, "get with the program," right? Somewhat.

But where we were ambushed was in letting despair creep in as the months rolled by without our finding that perfect placement. All that time, God's love and peace within us were not "keeping our hearts in perfect peace." Far from it, we rushed around trying to make things happen and despaired repeatedly when nothing happened. Four years of nothing is a long time! Four years without God's love and peace keeping our hearts made it seem even longer. Our Lord was "willing us not to despair," but we were defeating ourselves by our worry and attempted self-sufficiency. We prayed. We tried to rely on the Lord, but we failed miserably at letting our everlasting Keeper keep our hearts in love and peace.

So how do we access God's love and peace, which would guard us from despair? I've thought a lot about this, and I believe the answer is simple—not easy but simple. We discipline our minds to think about God's love, to meditate on the peace God gives instead of remembering our failings. *What we think is who we are.* If we think peaceful thoughts, we are peaceful. If we think on God's love, we know that love will keep us afloat even on enemy seas.

Julian says, "Our Lord wants us to remember that He is the ground of our whole life in love." God is our everlasting Keeper and will keep us in love and peace. But we can destroy that love and peace by worrying and by trying to handle life on our own. Test this in your own life. When an enemy approaches, what thoughts enter your head first—*God's love will keep me through this* or *What am I going to do?*

Julian's word to us is this: We fail when we rely on ourselves instead of our Lord. ❧

Reflection

1. To what areas of your life would the Lord say: "I wish you wouldn't despair over this. I will help you."?

2. What is your honest, inner response when you hear Julian say that your failures don't diminish the Lord's love for you? Can you truly believe that truth and rejoice in it?

3. What evidence do you have that God's love and peace are living and available inside you?

4. What are your worst "enemies"? How do you fight them?

5. What does it mean to you to have an "everlasting Keeper"? How does God keep you? What matter might God want to help with that you have tried to handle on your own?

Scripture

- Psalm 90
- Psalm 91
- John 14:25-27
- Isaiah 26:3-4

Exercise

List in your journal some times the Lord has rescued you from "enemies" (within and without). The next time you see an "enemy" approaching, relive these memories to remind yourself of God's love and faithfulness.

Mercy

*M*ercy is a sweet, gracious work of love, mingled with plenteous compassion. Mercy works in keeping us, and mercy works to turn all things into good. Mercy, by love, accompanies us when we fail. . . . Our failing is dreadful, our falling is shameful, . . . but in all this, the sweet eye of mercy and love is never absent, nor does mercy ever cease to work in us.

For I saw the nature of mercy, and it is the same as grace, both of which work through love. Mercy is a characteristic of the Motherhood [Christ]. Tender love and grace are divine characteristics of our royal Lord's love for us. Mercy works: keeping, accompanying, helping, and healing; and all this is tender divine love. And grace works: lifting us up, rewarding us, and endlessly surpassing all that we long for or deserve. Grace spreads abroad, showing the immensity of God's royal Lordship and marvelous courtesy flowing from abundant love. Grace works our dreadful failing into plenteous, endless solace; and grace works our shameful falling into soaring worship; and grace works our sorrowful dying into holy, blissful life.[8]

My most vivid experience of mercy took place on a retreat in the Australian bush. Retreat participants were asked to read through the Book of Matthew overnight and then go back to those passages where God drew us. On my first read-through, I was arrested by the story of the two blind beggars (see Matthew 20:29-34). They were sitting by the road shouting, "Lord, have mercy on us, Son of David!" The crowd told them to be quiet, but they continued shouting until Jesus stopped to listen. Verse 34 says, "Moved with compassion [mercy], Jesus touched their eyes. Immediately they regained their sight and followed him."

Next we were asked to return to a meaningful passage and imagine ourselves in it. I imagined Jesus looking at me with eyes of mercy, asking, "What do you want me to do for you?" (v. 32). I could see the love and mercy he felt for me. I dissolved in a healing stream of mercy. I am still unable to describe how it felt, but I knew that I was experiencing mercy as I had never done before and would never doubt again. I still feel warm and loved every time I recall this merciful experience.

As Christians, we often use words we can define but have never experienced. Experiencing God's grace is far different from simply knowing its meaning. The same is true of God's mercy and God's love. In this excerpt Julian tries to define *mercy, grace,* and *love* so that we can recognize and apprehend them.

"Mercy works . . . to turn all things into good," says Julian. She describes it as a sweet, gracious working. We have nothing to fear in mercy or grace; they are attributes of love that always benefit us. We may fear God's discipline or will for our lives, but we needn't fear mercy's sweet work, because it always brings good.

I picture mercy as something liquid, flowing over me like lotion for sunburn—taking the sting out of my circumstances and my hurting spirit. The sunburn may remain, but it doesn't burn with intense heat any more. God daily pours out mercy on our lives and our needs. So why don't we soak it in?

I talked about this experience of mercy with my spiritual director, Jill. She said we must use spiritual eyes to see this stream of mercy flowing over our lives. I remember questioning the presence of such mercy in a corrupt society. She shocked me by saying: "Kathy, there's mercy flowing down Collins Street!" (a major street in Melbourne). I stared in disbelief—until I thought about it. If we believe God's love is everywhere, then of course God's mercy is omnipresent too. Just as we need faith to believe in God and spiritual eyes to see God's love in action in this world, so too can we trust that our world is steeped in God's mercy.

How do we appropriate mercy for our needs? We do it in two ways:

1. *Make a habit of asking for mercy.* Now I often pray, "Lord Jesus Christ, have mercy on me." When I am in distress, I lie down and quietly repeat this prayer. It always calms my ruffled spirit and enables me to cope.

2. Ask God to help you see divine mercy in your situation. Believe that mercy exists, and better yet, actively look for it in a specific situation. When you are in pain, ask God to show you the divine working and places where mercy is saturating people and events with divine presence.

Jesus, in mercy, asks: "What do you want me to do for you?" Tell him. ❧

Reflection

1. Can you recall a time when you experienced God's mercy? If so, sit quietly and relive that experience. What was mercy like in that experience?

2. In what situation or relationship do you need mercy's balm in your soul?

3. Look at the actions of mercy in paragraph two of Julian's excerpt and apply those verbs to your needs. How does mercy "keep" you?

4. Do you agree with Julian that mercy is a characteristic of motherhood? How is this true in your life?

5. How might God's mercy be accompanying you in your life right now?

Scripture

• Ephesians 2:4-7
• Psalm 119:156
• Lamentations 3:22-26
• Luke 1:76-79

Exercise

Look up several more scriptures on mercy until you find one especially meaningful to you. Memorize it and carry it with you daily to help you become more aware of God's mercies. Write the verse on a card or piece of paper and slip it into your purse or briefcase.

Three Gifts of God

*T*hese revelations were shown to a simple, uneducated creature [woman] in the year of our Lord 1373, on the thirteenth day of May. This woman desired three gifts of God. The First was mind of [Christ's] Passion, the Second was bodily sickness in youth, at thirty years of age, and the Third was to have by God's gift three wounds.

As to the First, I thought I had some feeling in the Passion of Christ, but yet I desired more by the grace of God . . . I desired a bodily sight wherein I might have more knowledge of the bodily pains of our Saviour and of the compassion of our Lady [Mary] and of all His true lovers that saw . . . His pains. For I would be one of them and suffer with Him. . . .

The Second came to my mind with contrition . . . In this sickness I desired to have all manner of pains bodily and ghostly that I should have if I should die, . . . except the outpassing of the soul. And this I meant for [that] I would be purged, by the mercy of God, and afterward live more to the worship of God because of that sickness.

For the Third [petition], . . . I conceived a mighty desire to receive three wounds in my life: . . . the wound of very contrition, the wound of kind compassion, and the wound of steadfast longing toward God.

The first two desires dwindled, but the third dwelled with me continually.[9]

Imagine that an angel appeared before you and offered to grant you three wishes from God. What would you request? Freedom from some problem? Salvation for a family member? Healing of some sort? What do you need from God?

Would any of Julian's wishes appear on my list? I don't think so. I have spent most of my life trying to avoid pain. I don't even like to see dead animals by the roadside, so dwelling on Christ's painful death would not be one of my requests.

For us to understand Julian's requests, we must try to think like devout fourteenth-century Christians. Meditation on Christ's passion and death was a major means of bringing about repentance and becoming more Christlike.

As for Julian's asking for a serious illness, I can hardly comprehend why she might have made such a request. Two thoughts occur to me. One is that she wanted God to test her, and to her this would be the supreme test. The other is that she wanted to identify with Christ's suffering by experiencing illness herself. While this request appears extreme to us, Julian's desire to understand what Christ suffered is astounding.

Now, the three "wounds" come closer to appearing on my wish list. *Contrition* is not a word we hear often. It means "deep sorrow and repentance for sin." Not often do we hear—even in church—of deep sorrow over sins, nor do we practice contrition. But Julian deeply longed to mourn her sins and continually repent of the pain they caused her Lord.

Why aren't we more contrite? Perhaps it's because "easy forgiveness" has been preached too freely in our churches. How long should we mourn our sins? What should be our prayer posture toward habitual sins? Julian's goal was to have no sin.

I can identify with Julian's request for the wound of compassion. I also want to be a person of compassion. Recently I told my daughters, ages twenty-six and eighteen, that if I were to list character traits I wanted them to have, compassion would top my list. But being a compassionate person takes more time than most of us want to devote. Listening compassionately is much slower than listening inattentively. And random acts of kindness don't normally appear on our to-do lists. The truth is, the tyranny of the urgent wins out most days over unscheduled, compassionate actions. Julian desired a "loving compassion." Here I can relate to her humanness, because compassion doesn't always come naturally to me; I have to work at it. Yes, this request ought to appear on my list.

Her third request was a steadfast longing for God. I can identify wholly with that request. I have longed for a deeper relationship with God for as long as I can remember. What a joy it would have been to have known Julian, to have talked about God together. She could be a soul mate for anyone who longs for more of God. Julian's life seemed to be one extended longing after God—she truly desired to become a woman after God's own heart. She said that her other requests waned, but this one stayed with her—as her life and writings testify.

What would you request from God? What do you think you simply can't live without? More important, what do you think God wants for you? 🕸

Reflection

1. If you could request three things from God, what would you ask?

2. Looking at these requests, what do they say of your priorities in life?

3. What do these requests indicate about your relationship with Christ?

4. Which of Julian's requests would also be yours?

Scripture

• 1 Kings 3:7-9
• Matthew 19:16-30
• Matthew 6:19-24
• Matthew 20:20-28

Exercise

Spend time meditating over one of the above scripture passages about requests made to God. Then ask the Lord what you most need. Instead of just choosing your own requests, let your requests arise from truths you glean from these passages. See if you can hear God's heartbeat for you and your spiritual growth.

Pleasing God

*T*he continually seeking soul pleases God greatly. . . . The seeking with faith, hope, and charity pleases our Lord, and the finding pleases our souls and fills them with joy. . . .

It is God's will that we have three things in our seeking: The first is that we seek earnestly and diligently, without laziness. . . . The second is that we abide steadfastly in God's love, without complaining or striving against God, to our life's end. . . . The third is that we trust in God mightily with all our faith. It is God's will that we know that God will appear suddenly and blissfully to all who love [God].[10]

Have you ever thought about what epitaph you would want to summarize your life? I would like mine to read: "A soul who continually sought God."

Julian said that a continually seeking soul pleases God. She ought to know, since she devoted her life to seeking God. She said we should seek with faith, hope, and charity. I assume this would mean that we:

- believe God's words,
- place our hope for the future in God alone,
- love God and others with all our hearts.

Surely this kind of life would please God. But how do we live a God-seeking life?

Julian suggests three aspects of pleasing God. First, *seeking God requires some effort.* Most of us would like to have a sublime relationship with God in five minutes per day or less. We love God and want intimacy with the Holy One, but we think the effort required takes too much time. We "have a life" that consumes our time. In part due to the fact that God cannot be seen, our relationship with God gets crowded out. What we can't see, we forget, and our souls suffer.

Seeking God requires daily effort. We must set aside time for prayer and meditation if we ever will experience intimacy with God—to know and please God. Ideally, time with God needs to be at the top of our priorities. If we make time with God a priority, not only will God be pleased, but also our lives will bear the fruit of transformation.

The second aspect of seeking is *abiding with God*, which could be defined as accepting what God does, even when we can't understand. As if this weren't hard enough, we are to wait on God without complaining! Anyone who has ever awaited an answer to a desperately desired prayer knows how *long* God can take. When we wait for what seems like forever without complaining or giving up, that must surely please God. I am not a good waiter; I want God to answer *now*. Abiding with God—waiting for God's timing without complaining—may be the hardest test of all. Julian said the waiting shall last for "but awhile." I wonder if waiting seemed slow even to her.

The third aspect of seeking God is *trusting in faith*. *Faith* is a vague word. But I know the difference between when I trust God with faith and when I try to pretend that I do. Sometimes when I pray, I am convinced that God will answer. Other times I struggle to muster up faith that the sun will rise tomorrow. Julian said that faith pleases God.

But how do we build faith? I've begun to think it's cumulative. We believe in God on one occasion, and God answers. We remember that the next time—and faith accumulates over the years of trusting. What do we trust? That God will always be faithful to the promises found in scripture. God's faithfulness builds our trust, and we offer our trust in response to the divine faithfulness. So each feeds the other, and faith grows through decades of believing.

What is the reward of this faith? Julian wrote that God "will appear suddenly and blissfully to all who love [God]." Whether that is suddenly on a daily basis or at the end of this age, either will be welcome to us who love the Lord, for we will finally possess all that we have sought.

❧

Reflection

1. Can you honestly say that you are continually seeking God? What evidence can you give either way?

2. On a scale of 1 to 10 (1 being lowest), how would you rate your effort in seeking God?

3. Can you "stick it out" in daily life without complaining about what God is or isn't doing?

4. What are the evidences of God's faithfulness in your life?

5. How important in your life is pleasing God? What evidence would you give?

Scripture

- 1 Chronicles 28:9
- 2 Chronicles 7:14; 15:2
- Psalms 105:4; 119:2
- Proverbs 8:17
- Isaiah 55:6
- Amos 5:4
- Matthew 6:33

Exercise

To try seeking God in a new way, choose a spiritual discipline like journaling, fasting, meditation, or silence and set a time each day to spend seeking God. Try this routine for a month and see what difference it makes in your trust in God.

Vain Affections

*Y*es, I saw that our Lord cares about the tribulations of his servants, having pity and compassion on each person. It is God's bliss [purpose] to bring them a different perspective—to free them for the very things the world would mock and scorn. He tries to spare us from the pomp and vain-glory of this wretched life. For what the world would praise [and thus make us proud], He would have us scorn and make us fit for heaven and everlasting bliss. For the Lord says: *I shall wholly break you of your vain affections and your vicious pride; and after that I shall gather you together and make you mild and meek, clean and holy, by oneing [uniting you] to me.*[11]

I wonder what kind of lifestyle Christ would live if he were an American today. Would he have e-mail? Would he eat out? Where would he go to church? What would he do for a living? In short, how much would he buy into our Western values? Perhaps a better question is, how much should we?

How easy it is to to impose Western values on scripture. We tend to overlay cultural values on our reading of the Bible, then claim that our lifestyle is biblically based. Of course our values are based on scriptural principles! After all, isn't America a "Christian" country? What would Julian say to us?

Julian lived in a simpler time. But even in her time, choices had to be made about lifestyle, use of money, prestige, and the values of giving and caring. Julian lived in a prayer cell attached to the Norwich Cathedral. Not only did she take a vow of poverty, but she also gave up her freedom of mobility to devote her life to prayer and being a spiritual director for others. What were her values? God's kingdom, prayer, worship, and building a sense of spiritual community.

What a model of living for others! What possible

vain affections could Julian have struggled with? In today's excerpt, she mentioned "pomp" [pride] and the "vain-glory of this wretched life" as the temptations the Lord has listed for her.

Why is pride unable to exist in heaven? Perhaps because it competes with the Lord for primacy. Perhaps because pride is all about *me* instead of focusing on God. Whatever the reason, pride must be eradicated before we are ready to go to heaven and enter into everlasting bliss.

Likewise, the "glories" of this life perish in heavenly realms. Whatever is valuable only in this life we need to hold lightly or perhaps not at all. And according to Julian, such things will not bring us bliss. On the contrary, they keep us from God's bliss. God's bliss is all about the presence of the Holy One, which is all we will need when we get to heaven. But what do we do about *now*, Lord?

God answers, "I shall wholly break you of your vain affections and your vicious pride." These words tend to make us want to flee in terror. We think, *Lord, you can have everything else, as long as you leave me*_____. (What is your bliss?)

But my experiences of being broken of vain affections have not involved the Lord ripping them out of my grasping hands. Instead, my desire for those things simply melted away until they no longer meant anything to me. When I realize that God is trying to make me aware of any vain affection, I open my hands and offer up my "toys" with this attitude: "Lord, you are free to take anything out of my hands that does not please you."

Consider the rewards for giving up vain affections. Julian said that God will "make you mild and meek, clean and holy." Isn't the prize of true holiness more desirable than a few earthly toys? How will our gracious Lord accomplish this holiness in us? By "oneing" us with himself.

I love this word of Julian's—*oneing*—becoming one with the Lord. When we are oned with God, we desire what God desires; our affections become synonymous with God's affections.

Maybe it's time to give up your vain affections. Maybe it's time to look into scripture to see what God loves and to be "oned" with our Lord. ❧

Reflection

1. List your "vain affections." (Get started by listing where your discretionary money goes: clothes, chocolate, crafts? Or maybe it's prestige or career or a relationship. Which of these things does not include or honor God?)

2. In what areas of your life has God been nudging you to give up some vain affection? How have you responded?

3. What are you proudest of? How is this pride evidenced? How might it affect your spiritual life?

4. When have you tasted the Lord's bliss?

5. What keeps you from being "oned" with your Lord?

Scripture

- 1 John 2:15-17
- Mark 7:18-23
- Matthew 6:19-24
- Matthew 19:16-26

Exercise

Spend some time journaling on the topic of your most dearly held "vain affection." What about it holds you in its grasp? Do you master it, or does it master you? Dialogue with the Lord about this. What is an eternal perspective on this affection?

Royal Appointment

*H*e gave me understanding of two parts [of truth]. The one part is our Saviour and our salvation. This blessed part is open and clear and fair and light, and plenteous—for all [humanity] that is of good will. . . . Hereto are we bounden of God, and drawn and coun- selled and taught inwardly by the Holy Ghost and outwardly by Holy Church in the same grace. In this our Lord wills that we be occupied, joying in Him; for He enjoyeth in us. The more plenteously that we take of this, with reverence and meekness, the more thanks we earn of Him and the more speed to ourselves, thus, may we say, enjoying *our* part of our Lord. The other [part] is hid and shut up from us: that is to say, all that is beside our salvation. For it is our Lord's privy counsel, and it belongeth to the royal lordship of God to have His privy counsel in peace, and it belongeth to His servant, for obedience and reverence, not to learn wholly His counsel. Our Lord hath pity and compassion on us for that some creatures make themselves so busy therein; and I am sure if we knew how much we should please Him and ease ourselves by leaving it, we would.[12]

In this passage Julian picks up on a theme seldom heard in Christian teaching—that salvation is not just for heaven someday, but also for enjoying God here and now. She speaks to us of what God has revealed about salvation, calling this knowledge of salvation "the blessed part." She describes salvation as "open and clear and fair and light, and plenteous." How inviting!

Where does knowledge of salvation come from? Julian tells us that the Holy Spirit draws us to God, counsels us, and teaches us inwardly. The Spirit speaks to us, revealing God to us individually. But salvation is not an end in itself; there is more. God's plan for salva- tion indeed reveals God's nature to us. The purpose of this revelation is both for our knowledge of God and our relationship with God.

Julian stresses that salvation is all about enjoying God,

for God enjoys us. I wish I had heard this message decades ago in church—not the duty I owe God, but the joy of living my life with God. How my spiritual life has changed since I began to understand that the Christian life is about this love relationship—actually enjoying God.

The idea that God enjoys me was just as revolutionary. Salvation is the door through which we enter this relationship of mutual enjoyment. I can incorporate my enjoyment of God into my appreciation of nature or work or people—or anything. Quite simply, my relationship with God becomes my life—the center around which everything else revolves.

But the other aspect Julian wants us to remember is that we can never fully know God. Mystery is always present in our relationship with God. Why? Because God refuses to share God-self with us? More likely, the reason is that our finite minds cannot contain all of God. We are, after all, creatures in relationship with the Creator. Our task is to love all we can understand of God with all we know of ourselves. ❧

Reflection

1. What has been your understanding of salvation: as a means or an end?

2. What aspect of enjoyable relationship with God appeals to you most?

3. How have you been drawn, counseled, and taught by the Holy Spirit?

4. What of the mysteries of an infinite God intrigues you most?

5. Have you offered all you know of yourself to all you understand of God?

Scripture

- Psalm 16
- Romans 11:33-36
- Isaiah 40:18-26
- Psalm 84

Exercise

Spend time meditating on how much of your relationship with God is duty and how much is enjoyment. Make a date with God just to be together and enjoy each other. Perhaps you could walk in a beautiful place or enjoy a cup of tea and some solitude.

He Is Our Clothing

*I*n this same time our Lord showed me a spiritual sight of His homely loving. I saw that God is everything that is good and comfortable for us: He is our clothing. In love He wraps us, clasps us to Him, and encloses us with His tender love. Why? So that He may never leave us. He is everything that is good for us.[13]

A fashion expert Julian was not, with her body clothed in a rough, wool habit. Yet there is something womanly about her conceiving of God as our clothing.

I love nice clothes. I prefer a classic look that never goes out of style, but my greatest criterion is comfort. I want to look tailored but feel comfortable. I think Julian and I might have liked the same type of clothes. She conceived of God as comfy, well-fitting clothes.

I love Julian's choice of words. I'm amazed that she would call God's loving "homely." By homely, she does not mean ugly but familiar and comfortable—like a pair of well-worn jeans. She says God's love for her feels familiar and tender—it requires no formality.

So what does it mean for God to be our clothing? First, Julian emphasizes the closeness of our Lord. He is as close as the clothing on our skin. To some of us this might be a disconcerting thought. Do we really want God that close—that intimate? Or would that feel a little tight-fitting?

Most of us live with a contradictory idea of where God is. We have been taught that God dwells inside us when we become Christians. We want that. At the same time, we have this hazy concept that God is "out there" somewhere. So we must settle the question: Do we live an internal life or an external one? Will we live an inner life—with God intimately enmeshed in who we are and what we do? Or do we prefer that God stay "out there" at a safe distance so his clothing doesn't constrict our freedom?

Julian obviously wants this close-fitting God. Stop for a moment and reflect:

Is God "in here" (inside me) or "out there"? Why? Is there anything that makes me uneasy about God being my clothing?

To illustrate her emphasis on the closeness of God's love, Julian uses three verbs: *wraps, clasps, encloses.* All three words are similar in meaning, but what distinctions might Julian make? To have God's love wrapped around us implies protection. We wrap shawls or coats or blankets around us to protect us from the cold. Just so might God's love protect us from the cold of aloneness.

For clothing to be clasped around us implies that it clings to us. The idea of God's love clinging to us brings comfort in times when we have little strength to cling to God. Similarly, to be enclosed makes us think of warmth and security, protection and peace. God's love for us is Julian's main theme, and no image portrays the intimacy of that love better than being clothed in God.

Julian also says that not only are we clothed in this love, but that God's love is everything good and comfortable for us. I wonder, which does she mean? Is God the only *good* in our lives? If so, are we then to shun the world and live as recluses (as she did)? No, this doesn't ring true to her thinking. . . . I believe she is saying that everything in life that is good comes from God. We can trust that if it's good, God is in it and in it for our good.

Eugene H. Peterson, in *The Message*, paraphrases Christ's yoke as one that is neither "heavy" nor "ill-fitting." In his paraphrase, Christ invites us to keep company so we can "learn to live freely and lightly." Living freely and lightly sounds much like Julian's comfortable clothing.

Does your relationship with God through Christ fit comfortably? Or is it heavy and ill-fitting? Ponder the aspects that are comfortable and those that don't fit. ❧

Reflection

1. How comfortable do you feel with the concept of God being as close as your clothing?

2. Is God "in here" (intimate and comfortable) or "out there" (distant and less involved)?

3. When you pray, do you sometimes feel the need to be formal and "get it right," or do your prayers communicate a familiar intimacy, such as if you were talking with a close friend?

4. Picture God as your clothing. What sort of clothes are you wearing?

Scripture

- Matthew 11: 28-30 (my favorite version of this passage is in *The Message*)
- Romans 13:14
- Psalm 30:11-12
- Isaiah 61:10
- Galatians 3:27

Exercise

Practice seeing God in everything good around you by choosing some everyday object to prompt you to remember God's goodness and nearness—for example, telephone poles, which remind you of the cross, thus reminding you of God's love for you.

Fatherhood, Motherhood, Lordship

*A*nd I saw the working of all the blessed Trinity: in which I understood these three properties: God as Father, Christ as Mother, and the Holy Spirit as Lord, in one God.

In our Father Almighty we have our keeping and our bliss as part of our God-given nature. This is what it means to be made in the image of God.

And in the Second Person [Jesus], . . . are we restored and saved: for he is our Mother, Brother, and Savior.

And in our good Lord, the Holy Ghost [Spirit], we are rewarded and given mercy for our living and our troubles, endlessly surpassing all we could desire by his marvelous courtesy and His high plenteous grace.

For all our life is in three: in the first we have our Being, in the second we have our Increasing, and in the third we have our Fulfilling. The first is Nature, the second is Mercy, and the third is Grace.[15]

How did a fourteenth-century woman come up with the concept of the motherhood of Christ? She was an anchorite attached to a great cathedral in an era when men ruled. Yet Julian conceived of God as parents: father, mother, and Holy Spirit.

In grappling with the concept of the Trinitarian nature of God, Julian chose a familiar concept to aid our understanding of the fullness of God's nature.

The fatherhood of God is most familiar to us, but, as usual, Julian adds a new twist. She sees in God's fatherhood our keeping and our bliss. In Julian's day, *keeping* referred to provision—in this case, God's providential care for us. God the Father provides all of our physical needs: food, shelter, clothing, family, and all the other essentials. He is the ultimate father, tenderly providing for the well-being of every family member.

But Julian also describes God's fatherhood as our

"bliss." God was Julian's life, her joy, her bliss. She implies here that our real purpose on earth is to have a relationship with God. This relationship is also our bliss.

While God is clearly Father for Julian, God in Jesus is also Mother. What does Christ as a mother do? He restores and saves us. Restoring sounds very much like nurturing. Mothers often restore skinned knees, sagging spirits, and energy levels. All of those tender characteristics we associate with mothers caring for our "little" needs in life fit well into this picture of Christ as mother.

But Jesus as mother also saves us from our sins. We couldn't do that for ourselves, and Jesus lovingly took our punishment on the cross for our sins. Doesn't that sound like something a mother would do—give her life to save one of her children? Julian seems to think so. She calls Jesus "our Mother, Brother, and Savior."

And to the Holy Spirit, Julian assigns rewarding, giving mercy for daily living, and continually surpassing our expectations in giving grace for our every need. I would love to hear more of how Julian understood the Holy Spirit to be rewarding us in this life. Did she mean rewards for faithfulness, crowns in heaven, or simply blessings? Any or all of these definitions please me.

I like to think of the Holy Spirit as the personality of Jesus left behind in spirit form. Christ's body was gone, but his spirit remained in some mysterious form to guide and bless us. The Holy Spirit's job is to help us with daily living—giving mercy in our troubles, says Julian.

"For our life is in three," says Julian. In God the Father we have our Being. Whether or not we acknowledge God, God is still the one who gives us our life and our image that reflects the image of God. Colossians 3:3 says our life is "hidden with Christ in God." I think this is precisely what Julian wants us to remember. Our real life, our real selves are birthed and sustained by our relationship with God. This is our nature, who we are meant to be.

Our Being is in God, and our "Increasing" comes through Christ, our mother. Our well-being and our spiritual growth come through the nurture of this Christ-mother who tends and nurtures us. And it is mercy that nourishes and "increases" us.

Our "Fulfilling," then, is completed by the Spirit. Our desires and ambitions, both spiritual and temporal, are fulfilled by the Spirit. And this is accomplished by the abundant grace of God. Grace comforts in time of need and refines us when we need reining in.

What can this understanding say to us but that God is *all*, knowing our needs before we ask and amply providing everything in this amazing Trinity of Godhood. ◁

Reflection

1. To which of the three persons of the Trinity do you most often relate? Have you ever considered why?

2. What does God as Father mean to you? Is this a positive connection for you, or does it stir up negative associations?

3. How do you respond to Julian's thought of Christ as Mother? What images does this create for you?

4. What is your mental picture of the Holy Spirit? Do you ever pray to the Holy Spirit? Why or why not?

5. Think about the ways that you experience the mercy and grace of God.

Scripture

- Psalm 131
- Psalm 91
- John 14
- Matthew 23:37-39

Exercise

Take some opportunity to observe a mother with her child. Note her tender nurture, then mentally apply that mothering to Christ. Allow Christ to restore those empty spaces in you that crave a mother's tender, loving care.

All crimes, hatred, cruelty,

and every kind of evil

are rooted in self-love,

which poisons

the whole world

and weakens

the church.

—CATHERINE OF SIENA

Meet Catherine of Siena

Catherine was born the next to last of twenty-five children in a wool dyer's family in Siena, Italy, in 1347. She seems to have known Christ from an early age. At age six, she had a vision of Christ dressed in papal robes and surrounded by saints; Christ smiled and blessed her but said nothing.

At age seven, Catherine vowed to remain a virgin, and she dedicated her virginity to Christ. After her favorite sister died in 1362, Catherine devoted herself to prayer and solitude. Her mother urged her to marry, but fifteen-year-old Catherine objected, even cutting off her hair to make herself less attractive. She quarreled a great deal with her parents, and because she refused to follow their wishes for her, her parents began treating her as a servant. When another sister died a year later, Catherine began the practice of fasting, a discipline that would persist throughout her life. About that time, she became fascinated with a group of devout Dominican women. At first they did not care for Catherine because she seemed overly pious and withdrawn. But after she persisted, they gave her permission to become a member of their group.

Catherine was eighteen when she joined the Third Order of Dominicans. This order was made up of laypeople who were allowed to live at home instead of in a cloister; they actively ministered to the outside world. But Catherine shut herself away in her home for three years, going out only for Mass and confession. During this time she learned to read and developed many ascetic habits (habits of self-denial). She practiced strict fasting, eating little food except the Eucharist. Catherine claimed that she received her physical sustenance from spiritual food. (The story is also told that she sobbed loudly every time she took Communion, disturbing others in attendance.) The only person she spoke to was the priest who heard her confessions. She survived on just two hours of sleep per night. Her self-flagellation and desire to suffer for Christ seem extreme to us. Nevertheless, her time of solitude and prayer served as the foundation for her great spiritual power and her life's work.

In the summer of 1368, at age twenty-one, Catherine experienced a mystical espousal to Christ. She continued to have mystical experiences of increasing intensity. Another climactic point was her mystical death, which occurred in 1370, that left her in a long, deathlike trance. During this four-hour ecstatic experience, according to witnesses, Catherine appeared to have stopped breathing. She awoke praying and declared that she was now united with Christ.

After her mystical death experience, Catherine felt God's call to abandon her life of solitude and become active in ministering to the world. She nursed the sick, helped the poor, and soon gained a reputation for having great spiritual wisdom. People flocked to her for spiritual counsel. They were drawn by Catherine's gaiety, friendliness, common sense, serenity, and spiritual insights.

About this time, a severe crisis erupted in the church because of the pope's leaving Rome to live in Avignon, France, some seventy years earlier. Since the papacy had moved to Avignon, the Italian church had been in almost constant strife with the French papal legates. Finally in 1376 Florence declared war on the papal states to protest their rule. Within ten days eighty other towns joined Florence in the dispute. Acting as an ambassador for the Florentines, Catherine journeyed to Avignon to try to convince Pope Gregory XI to return the papal headquarters to Rome. Eventually the pope heeded her advice and returned to Rome in 1377.

Catherine spent most of 1377 in evangelistic efforts that resulted in a great spiritual revival in the districts around Siena. At Pope Gregory's request, she returned to Florence early in 1378 as an ambassador, trying to reconcile a dispute between the pope and the church leaders of Florence. After she succeeded in resolving the quarrel (by this time there was a new pope), Catherine returned to Siena for a few months, where she dictated her book *The Dialogue of Saint Catherine*.

The Dialogue tells of Catherine's visions and other spiritual experiences, as well as giving instructions for cultivating a life of prayer. Much of the book is written in the form of informal conversations between God and a human soul (represented by Catherine).

Catherine spent the last eighteen months of her life in Rome, alternating between helping the poor and sick and working to reform the church. She literally gave her life to the cause of Christ—whether she was nursing the sick, helping the poor, or preaching the gospel. In January 1380, she suffered a stroke while dictating a letter to the pope. Then in April, she suffered another stroke while praying at Saint Peter's. Catherine died several days later at age thirty-three, finally and fully "united with Christ."

What can we learn from her? Catherine provided a great example of ministry to the needs of others, devotion and passion for Christ, tireless work for the things she believed in, and courage as she took a strong stand on the issues of her time. In 1970 Pope Paul VI declared Catherine of Siena a Doctor of the Church for her many years of extraordinary effort on behalf of the church.

Come to Me and Drink

[Catherine hears God speak these words to her.]

*Y*ou were all invited, . . . by My truth, when Jesus cried out in the temple, saying "Whosoever thirsts, let that person come to Me and drink, for I am the Fountain of the Water of Life." Jesus did not say, "Go to the Father and drink." Rather, the invitation was, "Come to Me." He spoke thus because in Me, the Father, there can be no pain, but in My Son there can be pain. And you, while you are pilgrims and wayfarers in this earthly life, cannot be without pain. That is because this mortal life, through sin, brought forth thorns. We are invited to drink, then, because by following the doctrines of Jesus, whether in the most perfect way or by dwelling in the life of common charity, we drink of the fruit of the Blood of Jesus. In doing this we learn to live a life of charity and find union with the Divine nature.

As you find yourself in Jesus Christ, you also find yourself in Me, . . . the Sea Pacific, because I am one with My Son and He with Me. So you are invited to the Fountain of the Living Water of Grace. It is right for you, with perseverance, to keep close to my Son, who is a bridge for you that will keep you from being thrown by any wind, either of adversity or prosperity. Persevere till you find Me, . . . the Giver of the Water of Life, by means of this sweet and amorous Word, my only-begotten Son. He was the Fountain which contained Me, the Giver of the Living Water that enables union of the Divine with human nature. Therefore I made My Son the bridge because no one can pass through this life without pain, and in Him there can be pain. No one can come to Me except by [Jesus], the Bridge.

Now that you understand, persevere, otherwise you shall not drink, for perseverance receives the crown of glory and victory in the life everlasting.[1]

I'm teaching a New Testament course that includes a session on Greek gods. I find it fascinating that the Greeks (and Romans) had a god for every area of life. Zeus, the supreme god, controlled the sky, the weather, and fate. Demeter was a grain goddess, responsible for the success of crops—the mainstay of the Roman diet.

Artemis was the goddess of hunters (again a survival issue), childbirth, and death. Poseidon was the god of the sea, earthquakes, and horses. Aphrodite was the love goddess; Hestia, the goddess of the hearth; and Dionysus the god of wine. In reality these gods controlled nothing—they were merely an explanation for why things happened. For example, if a thunderstorm struck, people believed that Zeus was angry with them.

Because the Greeks and Romans based their beliefs on circumstances, the purpose of their worship was to placate the gods and coerce them into a favorable mood. I cannot comprehend how intelligent people pretended to feed statues of their gods, wash them, and talk to them. Such behavior seems more like a child playing with dolls than worship. But the huge hole I see in the Greek and Roman concept of gods is any concept of a loving supreme being who desired a personal relationship with them.

What a wonderful contrast, then, is our God, who invites us through Jesus Christ, "Let anyone who is thirsty come to me, and let the one who believes in me drink" (John 7:37-38). What sets our God apart from gods that humans created? We can't see our God, but we know that the Almighty became human in the person of Jesus Christ, dwelt among us, and understands our pain. Furthermore, our God speaks to us through scripture and even speaks directly to our hearts—if only we will listen. We worship a living, loving God who longs for a relationship with each of us—and is the fountain that can satisfy all our thirsts.

What is so appealing about a fountain? Fountains were originally sources of daily water supply. Without indoor plumbing in their homes, people often went to fountains to slake their thirst in a hot, arid climate. The closest comparison that we have is a drinking fountain. But where can we go to satisfy our real thirsts in life—emotional and spiritual thirsts?

Jesus invites us to come to the *real* Fountain of life, which satisfies all our needs completely. That Fountain is Jesus, who knows our needs because he lived as a human and therefore understands how painful and "thirsty" life can be.

Ours is not a god who doesn't know our pains or care. Jesus not only suffered pain—but even suffered it on our behalf! He went a step further and conquered pain and death. Why? So that we would not have to suffer alone. We can go to our Fountain again and again and find grace and help in time of need. The water in this Fountain is grace—grace sufficient not only for our sins but also for all our emotional and spiritual pain in this painfully finite life.

The grace flowing from this Fountain enables me to persevere when I couldn't otherwise. Whenever I feel like I can't go on, I ask the Lord to pick me up and carry me. (I once had a beautiful print of Jesus the Shepherd. Sheep were clustered around his feet, and one lamb was safely sheltered in his arms. I would look at that lamb and say, "Jesus, pick me up and carry me like that little lamb. I can't make it on my own." Nothing dramatic happened, but sometime later I would look back and realize that I *had* made it through the difficult time. And then I'd realize that the grace of Jesus had carried me, easing my way.) In order to persevere, we need the grace that only Jesus can give.

As we persevere, something else happens. We are being united with the divine. We are becoming more Christlike, and generally we like ourselves more and more. Becoming more like Christ is who we most want to be, if only we can persevere long enough to realize that. How long must we persevere? Until we receive the "crown of glory and victory in the life everlasting," Catherine says. Perseverance in this life wins us eternal life and all its rewards, which are beyond our wildest imagining. So the invitation "come to Me, and . . . drink" is for this life and the next! ❧

Reflection

1. What do you thirst for spiritually—what do you really want from God?

2. How do you respond emotionally to Christ's invitation, "Come to me"?

3. Describe your present relationship with God and how it compares to the type of relationship you desire.

4. What helps you persevere in life's hard places? What are your greatest obstacles?

5. Does the thought of union with God frighten you? Why or why not?

Scripture

• Isaiah 55:1-3
• Matthew 11:25-30
• Romans 5:1-11
• John 17
• 1 Corinthians 16:13-14

Exercise

If you keep a journal, read back through a section that describes a difficult time for you. If you do not journal, try to remember some time when you were experiencing struggle and discouragement. What helped you persevere then? Did you sense God saying anything to you? What practices did you use to stand firm in your faith and in your witness? Most important, how have you grown through that painful experience?

The Virtue Tree

[Catherine hears God speak these words to her.]

A life of virtue demonstrates that the will is dead, continually slain by attacking selfishness and sensuality. . . . This virtue of discretion [wisdom or discernment] is equivalent to a true knowledge of oneself and of Me, and in this knowledge is virtue rooted. Discretion, or wisdom, is the only child of self-knowledge and, combined with love, has many other descendants, like a tree with many branches.

But that which gives life to the [virtue] tree, to its branches, and its root is the ground of humility, in which [the tree] is planted. Humility is the foster-mother and nurse of charity, by whose means this tree remains in the perpetual calm of discretion [wisdom]. Otherwise the tree could not produce the virtue of discretion, or any fruit of life, if it were not planted in humility, because humility proceeds from self-knowledge.

And I have already said to you, that the root of discretion is a real knowledge of self and of My goodness, by which the soul immediately, and discreetly, renders to others whatever they need. The virtuous soul primarily offers praise and glory to My name, and this soul sees and knows that the gifts and graces it has received come from Me. This soul recognizes where the credit for its successes lies—not in itself, but in Me. This soul knows well that it cannot even exist on its own—that all of life is a gift of grace from Me.

Catherine's original sentences have many confusing clauses and go on for lines and lines. Decoding her central thought often challenges even determined readers. This passage is full of metaphors and virtues, but even the most cursory reading clearly portrays Catherine's passion for a virtuous life.

Catherine chooses the image of a tree to describe how virtues are interrelated. So let's imagine a cherry tree like one you might see on a sampler. Its overall shape is circular, and its appearance is vibrant. When we look more closely at this tree, we notice that the "cherries" are actually virtues. Some of the cherry-red virtues are wisdom, discernment, and charity. We spy sturdy branches laden with fruit bursting with self-knowledge and knowledge of God's goodness. The virtue tree stands tall and vibrant, rooted in humility.

The word *humility* originates from the Latin word *humus*, meaning earth. As we step back to admire the virtue tree, we long to pick its luscious, tempting fruit. Surely it resembles the fruit tree that tempted Eve in the Garden!

Catherine's message for us in this image is that godly virtues are indeed interrelated. Pursuing one virtue leads us to other virtue clusters. We cannot attain discernment apart from self-knowledge or knowledge of God; neither can we attain charity apart from humility. But why should this be so? Because our Lord embodies all the virtues in one source—Godself. So then, attaining virtues implies a momentum—we are either moving toward a virtue network or away from them.

So where do we begin? Catherine repeatedly tells us that spiritual growth begins with self-knowledge, or a true assessment of ourselves. Let's look at this quote in reverse order. In the last paragraph Catherine succinctly describes two traits of self-knowledge.

1. *Self-knowledge involves recognizing that we are nothing on our own.* We can do nothing on our own; everything we accomplish is by a gift of grace. Acknowledging this truth leads to humility.

2. *Humility expresses itself in praise to God and charity toward others.* In some Christian circles, humility has degenerated into a sort of sickening self-deprecation. But Jesus was never self-deprecating. On the contrary, Jesus constantly acknowledged his kinship with God, but that kinship was characterized by love, not abuse of power.

True humility arises from a keen sense of who we are in Christ—in both our God-given strengths and our human weaknesses. We may know ourselves as competent, intelligent women but also human and fallible women. Yes, we are both—that is the human condition.

I believe that accepting our weaknesses as part of our identity is the key to humility and, thus, to greatness (or a virtuous life, as Catherine calls it). We must never lose our focus on Christ: Humility, then, is the root that nurtures every other virtue on our virtue tree.

Out of humility grows discernment (Catherine uses the word *discretion*), from which we rightly view ourselves and others. We are not inferior to others, nor are we superior to them. We are all in this human condition together—for our mutual benefit!

Charity, Catherine says, is the natural result of humility. Our charity—compassion toward others—springs from the knowledge that we are all needy and that we are here to help one other. Virtues are not an end in themselves; they are the means to living a godly life in Christian fellowship.

One last word about a virtuous life: We often get caught up in the effort required to live a virtuous life for the benefit of others. But let's never forget that virtuous living is reciprocal. We receive compassion, charity, and consideration from others who are working at living a virtuous life on our behalf! The virtue tree's fruits nourish us all. ❧

Reflection

1. Do you ever grow weary of trying to live a virtuous or holy life? Why do you suppose this happens? Have you ever noticed any cause-and-effect patterns?

2. What virtue or virtues do you greatly desire? Why?

3. Think of a woman who exemplifies humility. Can you define what humility looks like in her life?

4. Do you often compare yourself with others? How do you most frequently see yourself—as inferior or superior to them?

5. How well do you know your own weaknesses—or do you hide from acknowledging them?

Scripture

• 1 Corinthians 1:18-31
• Proverbs 11:2
• Proverbs 17:24, 27
• 1 Corinthians 13
• 1 Peter 1:3-12

Exercise

Today's exercise is designed to help you capture in writing some knowledge of yourself. Make a list of your skills and gifts. Thank God for these gifts of grace.

Now make a list of your weaknesses, dividing them into two categories: personality traits and results of your environment. Thank God for your weaknesses, asking for healing and grace to accept them as well as your strengths. Ask God to help you learn true humility.

Sinning against Your Neighbor

[Catherine hears God speak these words to her.]

*T*hose who do not love . . . injure themselves, for they cut themselves off from grace, and injure their neighbors, by depriving them of the benefit of prayers and all that would bind them to Me. . . . If these persons do not love Me, they cannot live in charity with their neighbors. Thus all evil comes from a lack of love for Me and for one's neighbor. . . . You are obliged to help your neighbor by word and doctrine and through the example of good works and in every other respect in which your neighbor is in need. . . .

I have told you how all sins committed against Me are committed against your neighbor. Mainly this is done by depriving others of love, the chief of virtues. In the same way, self-love destroys love toward your neighbor and is the foundation of every evil. All scandals, hatred, cruelty, and every kind of evil are rooted in self-love, which poisons the whole world and weakens the church.

Therefore, I say to you that it is in loving your neighbor that all other virtues are born. Love gives life to all the virtues, because no virtue is possible without love, the pure love that comes from Me. . . .

It cannot be otherwise, for love of Me and love of your neighbor are one and the same. As you love Me, so will you love your neighbor, because love toward your neighbor issues from Me. So this is how you prove your virtue: since you can't do anything tangible for Me, do it for others instead. This proves that you possess Me by grace in your soul. . . . The soul, enamored of My truth, never ceases to serve the world.

Catherine's words here make us squirm. We like to think that we live virtuous lives. After all, we serve our families, our churches, our communities. We live clean, wholesome lives and even tithe! But Catherine says that when we don't love our neighbors, we sin against God.

Loving and serving your neighbor are two different things. It is worlds easier to take a meal or write a check to charity than to love, especially people we don't know.

Through Catherine's writing God says to us: "If you don't show love toward your neighbor, you are sinning. It doesn't matter what your intentions are. Whether you think evil thoughts or act them out, it has the same effect."

Jesus loves each of us, and he hurts when we hurt. If someone sins against us, Jesus also feels the sin. But somehow this aspect of our being joined together in the body of Christ doesn't sink deeply into our consciousness. Christ sees all sin as corporate sin. Any sins we commit against each other are also sins against Christ, and they injure the body of Christ, the church.

How is it, then, that we so easily forget this interrelatedness? God tells Catherine here that it's due to the sin of self-love, or in our culture's language, self-centeredness. Our culture tells us, "Look out for Number One"—or look out for your own fulfillment. Thus we live individual lives and commit what we think are individual sins. And in so doing, we divide the body of Christ and deprive others of our love.

Old Testament believers had no concept of individual life or faith. To belong to God was to belong to a community that corporately sinned or served God. Remember Achan, who hid the spoils of battle, with the result that an entire nation was punished? (See Joshua 7.) God says we are in this together. It's not about me and my sin; it's about *us*—all of God's people together. God never intended for us to live our lives without the support *and* accountability of a community. We Americans have much to explain to the rest of the world for our individual lives of affluence in light of widespread hunger.

But wait a minute. Isn't this a little harsh, to say that we sin against others simply by not loving them? How can *not* loving someone we never met be called "sinning" against them? This is precisely how we rationalize our selfishness, ignoring the needs of others. Are we really honest when we rationalize that because we don't know the hungry of the world, we shouldn't love them? Sure, it's easier to love those whom we've met and "connected" with. But isn't that a selfish perspective— to decide that we will only love and help those whom we have met (and, by implication, approved)?

Catherine's words in this excerpt claim that all crimes are committed out of self-love—and all virtues stem from love of God. Herein lies our answer to the problem of self-love and our sinfulness. If our focus is on loving God, not ourselves, we will share that love with those around us. We will not deprive others of love simply because we are caught up in our own selfish ambitions.

It's a huge shift for our individualistic society to respond to the needs of persons we'll never meet and perhaps not receive tax credit for our donations. Every American needs to leave the comfort zone and visit a developing country. Then the needy have names and faces, and compassion naturally makes one want to love and help others. As Catherine said, "The soul, enamored of My truth, never ceases to serve the world."

Reflection

1. How is loving your neighbors related to loving God?

2. How is sinning against your neighbor related to sinning against God?

3. Do you feel connected to the body of Christ globally as well as locally?

4. Consider how you can love people you may never meet. Identify specific actions this kind of love might prompt.

5. In what ways do you experience interdependence with other people? What do you think Christ is teaching you about this?

Scripture

- Galatians 5:16-26
- Joshua 7
- Philippians 2:1-11
- 1 Corinthians 12
- Romans 12

Exercise

Spend time thinking about your interdependence with others around the world. How could you practically extend your concern and influence for the good of God's kingdom?

Loving for Personal Profit

[Catherine hears God speak these words to her.]

Some people serve Me faithfully and loyally, not out of fear of punishment but out of love. This very love, however, is imperfect if they serve Me out of desire for their own profit or even for the pleasure they find in Me. Do you know what proves the imperfection of this love? Occasionally, I withdraw the consolation they find in My presence. I allow them to fall into perplexities and trials in order to push them to rise above the mediocre levels of their imperfect love. This I do so that, when they come to perfect self-knowledge [see themselves as they really are], they may know that by themselves they are nothing and have no grace. Accordingly, in time of battle, they may fly to Me, their benefactor, for consolation and grace.

If they love me only for My consolation, when it is withdrawn, I see in them only weak love for their neighbors that often disappears entirely. At such times, these weak ones relax their energy, impatiently abandoning their spiritual disciplines. They tell themselves that they are not profiting from all the work involved in spiritual disciplines. All this they do because they feel deprived of My presence and consolation.

Such souls act imperfectly because they feel deprived of My presence and because they have not yet unwound the bandage of spiritual self-love. If they had, they would recognize that everything proceeds from Me. Not a leaf falls to the ground without My providence. Further, all that I promise and give to My children, I do out of My great love for them and My desire for their sanctification—which is the reason I created them. My children must see and know that I wish nothing but their good, through the Blood of My only-begotten Son, in which they are washed from their iniquities. . . . .But since they are imperfect, they use Me only for their own profit, relaxing their love.for their neighbor. Love cannot be based only on the desire for one's needs to be met.

Here is a tale of two friends from my past. Friend One was an intelligent professional woman. We shared common interests and happened into a friendship of sorts. I say "of sorts" because the friendship never became very deep. It didn't take me long to realize that our friendship was all about her. When we planned an outing, she chose where to go, where to eat, when to return. When we talked, our conversations centered on her life, her problems. She asked favors, she had needs. I was there to fulfill her friendship needs and other sundry needs as they arose. As you would expect, she had unresolved problems from her past that had left her self-absorbed and incapable of loving others. I listened, counseled, prayed—but it was never enough. I was finally released from this wearying relationship when my family moved.

Friend Two (Sandy) approached me for friendship and became a source of true joy. We shared a friendship of common interests, both professional and personal. She could never seem to do enough for me. She would learn of my plans and think three steps ahead to offer help I hadn't yet realized I needed. If she made jam, I was certain to receive a jar. If she was planning a trip into town, she offered to run errands for me. As we became better acquainted, I realized that she treated everyone this way. Her life was filled to overflowing with rich, intimate relationships because she was not in them to meet her own needs. Sandy loves people. She truly loves giving herself away—not in a sick, codependent manner but in a truly inspiring, selfless life.

These relationships also highlight two different kinds of friendship with our Lord. Let's go back to Friend One and examine her spiritual life. When she prays, it's all about her. She experiences no silence or adoration because she's too busy nagging God about her needs and her requests.

When life is going along fairly well, Friend One is occasionally able to serve God or others, but then her own needs overwhelm her again. She makes demands of God and others. When demanding doesn't work, she whines, accuses, and lays guilt trips on others so they will do what she wants. When these tactics don't work in her prayer life, she blames God for her troubles. And when God withdraws the sweetness of his presence out of a desire to stretch her, she gives up and withdraws into herself, sighing, "No one really understands me. Nobody loves me."

Can Friend One ever have a healthy, satisfying relationship with God? Anything is possible with God—but she needs somehow to get beyond her self-obsession. "Dying to self" is not an idle, biblical phrase. To be able to truly love God or anyone else, we must die to self.

What about Friend Two? Is her relationship with God always perfect? No, but Sandy knows how to worship and revel in God's presence. She doesn't waste time whining or badgering God. Even when God chooses to stretch her, she perseveres in her daily disciplines, secure in God's love for her. She does the right things for the right reasons and trusts that the sweet sense of God's presence will return. She knows she is nothing without the grace of God—and that the purpose of her life is to love and serve God and others. Her loving service to her neighbors indicates that she loves God greatly indeed.

I can look back to a difficult phase of my past and recognize myself as Friend One in that place and time. We all go through needy times and use others. But the real question is: Do we stay there?

I am learning that we are to love God for God's own benefit. I am also learning that life is not about me—but about living a life that pleases God (which automatically involves serving others). Slowly and painfully, I am dying to self. I want a life that makes God smile! ✍

Reflection

1. If your friends were honest, would they say you are more like Friend One or Friend Two? Why?

2. What tendencies of Friend One do you see in yourself? How will you try to change them?

3. What characteristics of Friend Two are you cultivating (by spiritual disciplines)?

4. How do you spend most of your prayer time?

5. How do you handle spiritual dry times? Do you relax your spiritual routines then—or increase them?

Scripture

• Hebrews 12:4-17
• Hosea 6:1-6
• Deuteronomy 7
• Nehemiah 9:5-15
• Revelation 3:1-6

Exercise

In your journal, list your friends in two categories: those like Friend One and those like Friend Two. Then list your characteristics that resemble those of Friend One and Two. Resolve to become more like Friend Two.

Taking Grace for Granted

[Catherine hears God speak these words to her.]

I wish you to know that, although I recreated and restored to the life of grace the human race through the Blood of My only-begotten Son, humans are not grateful, but are going from bad to worse, and from guilt to guilt. They take so little account of the grace which I have given them, and continue to give them, that not only do they not attribute what they have received to grace, but they sometimes even blame their injuries on Me—as if I had any wish for them but their sanctification!

I say to you that they will be more hard-hearted and worthy of more punishment now that they have received redemption through the Blood of My Son. . . .

Humans are closely bound to Me by the fact that I made them in My own image—I made them to glorify Me. But they chose to glorify themselves instead. Thus, in their disobedience, they became My enemies. But I redeemed them from this evil and from the devil's service by offering them redemption through the Blood of My Son. I made them free by my grace. . . . This is the debt they have incurred—the treasure of the Blood, by which they have been procreated to grace. See how much more they owe after redemption than before? Now they are obliged to render Me glory and praise by following in the steps of My only-begotten Son, for then they repay Me the debt of love both of Myself and of their neighbor, with true and genuine virtue.

Many parents can completely identify with the heartbreak of these words as they think about their own wayward children—children they raised lovingly and from whom they desire only love in return.

I thank God daily for our two wonderful daughters, both of whom love us and the Lord. Angela works with the disabled, helping them find jobs. Most days I receive an e-mail from her telling me she loves me. And Elizabeth, still in college, plans on giving her life to humanitarian work overseas. Both of them delight my heart as I think of the impact of their lives on our needy world. I am further blessed in the loving relationships we share. I cannot imagine how miserable Phil and I would have been if they had scorned the love and values that we tried to give them. Yet how many people treat God this way—disregarding the gracious redemption God offers? Worse yet, it appears that the words in Catherine's excerpt are directed to Christians.

How easily we get caught up in our hectic lives for months, forgetting to thank God for the marvelous gift of free salvation. As I write this meditation, it is Lent. Lent is meant to remind us of the great cost Christ paid for the salvation offered to us so freely.

Sin is not a popular word these days. What qualifies as sin? And who among us needs this costly redemption, bought by Christ's blood? Surely someone sinned to necessitate Christ's death on the cross. When we take lightly the sacrifice of the cross, we also deny ourselves the grace we so desperately need.

Worse yet, by rejecting God's word regarding our sins, we make God out to be the enemy. We begin to imagine that God is out to get us—that life's injuries are sent by God to punish us. Our (unconscious and irrational) reasoning goes something like this:

1. I believe that I can make it on my own.
2. I don't need God to tell me how to clean up my life.
3. I am doing the best I can, and God ought to know that.
4. It is unfair for God to accuse me of sin when I'm not responsible for _____.
5. If God really loved me, God would overlook this area of my life. I'll get it right eventually.
6. I don't think God could love me and do this to me.

Why is it so hard for us to admit that we are weak sinners in need of God's help? We've never gotten it right, and we never will on our own. Once we confront our own sins and confess them, we're given forgiveness and grace to live lives pleasing not only to us but to God as well.

So what is grace, and how is it manifested in our lives?

- Grace is what enables us to keep going on days when we long to quit life.
- Grace enables us to forgive when we have been wronged and long for revenge.
- Grace keeps our mouths shut on angry retorts we'd regret later.
- Grace accepts others when their unlovely behaviors offend us.
- Grace is how I accept myself with my own sins and weaknesses.
- Grace is much more than I could ever define—it is what makes life a pleasure, not a test.

An excerpt from Paul Tillich's writing reminds me that grace is free for the taking. Somehow God accepts me.

Grace strikes us when we are in great pain and restlessness. It strikes us when we walk through the dark valley of a meaningless and empty life. . . . when we feel that our separation is deeper than usual, . . . when despair destroys all joy and courage. Sometimes at that moment a wave of light breaks into our darkness, and it is as though a voice were saying: "You are accepted. *You are accepted,* accepted by that which is greater than you, the name of which you do not know. Do not ask for the name now; perhaps you will find it later. Do not try to do anything now; perhaps later you will do much. Do not seek for anything; do not perform anything; do not intend anything. *Simply accept the fact that you are accepted!*" If that happens to us, we experience grace.[2]

Christ purchased this grace for us with his blood. Once we confess our sins, we can stand before God, washed of our sins—accepted. And there's more—when we accept it, we are given abundant grace for living our lives in joyous partnership with the God who graciously gave the beloved Son, Jesus Christ, for us.

I used to wonder how to obtain grace. Then one day the realization hit me: I simply ask for it. When you need grace, ask and you will receive it! ✍

Reflection

1. When have you felt that God is hard on you? Why?

2. What unconfessed sin do you have in your life?

3. How do you define grace? What scriptures have helped you understand the meaning of grace?

4. How do you experience God's grace in your life now? How have you experienced God's grace in the past?

5. Do you sense God calling you to offer grace to some person or circumstance in your life?

Scripture

- 2 Corinthians 12:7-10
- John 1:1-16
- Hebrews 4:7-16
- Ephesians 2

Exercise

In your journal, list your sins and offer them up to God. Then make two lists: one of those people who have shown great grace to you; and the other, those people around you who need your gracious acceptance. Pray for them and ask the Lord to show you ways to pour grace into their lives.

Greedy Moles

[Catherine hears God speak these words to her.]

*C*ovetous misers, acting like moles, feed on the fruit of the earth all their lives. When they die, they find that death has no remedy for avarice [greed]. These greedy ones, with their meanness, despise My generosity, selling even to their neighbors. They cruelly use and rob their neighbors because they do not remember My mercy. If they understood mercy, they would not be cruel to themselves or to their neighbors. Instead, they would be compassionate and merciful to themselves, practicing the virtues on their neighbor and succoring him charitably.

Oh, how many are the evils that come from this sin of greed—how many homicides and thefts, and how much cruelty of heart and injustice! Greed kills the soul and makes her the slave of riches, so that she cares not to observe My commandments.

A miser loves no one except for her own profit. Greed proceeds from and feeds pride—they're inseparable. The miser is always consumed with her own reputation . . . and when greed is combined with pride, it goes from bad to worse. . . . It also produces a deceitful heart, which is neither pure nor generous. . . . Furthermore, it produces envy, which is a worm that is always gnawing, giving the miser no peace or happiness in what she already possesses. . . . Oh, miserable vices that destroy the heaven of the soul.

I confess that I have a greedy soul. I love flea markets, junk stores, and garage sales. There's something so satisfying about finding a great price on a "treasure" in a junk store. My best bargain ever is a Victorian quilt I found in a little antique store in rural Maryland. I spied it lying on the floor in a pool of antique satin and velvet. Its black satin background is divided in two with velvet fans. Then C. J. (whose initials are on the back) embroidered flowers onto the velvet fans. The quilt is a masterpiece from the 1880s. (We had recently stayed in a Victorian bed-and-breakfast for our anniversary, and I saw a quilt just like this on the wall.) My bargain price? Only ten dollars!

Was I greedy to take the quilt at that price without telling the shop owner that it was worth much more? Probably.

Catherine calls covetous people "moles" because they spend their lives eating dirt and have nothing to show for it in the end. Moles are also blind and can't even see what they are collecting. These words speak harshly to a consumeristic society that advises a shop-till-you-drop mentality. What other society offers counseling for shopping addictions?

And why do we buy? A better question is, why are we never satisfied?

Catherine (and scripture) calls greed a sin that separates us from a focus on God. She lists several unpleasant characteristics of the greedy woman. First, she says the greedy one is mean to her neighbors. How? By selling to them and robbing them. Surely we are not guilty of these crimes! But what about when we rob our neighbors of their reputations by spreading innuendoes and gossip? Or when we use them by borrowing things and returning them broken—or perhaps never returning them at all? As for homicides, thefts, injustice, and cruelty of heart—it is hard to believe that Christians would commit these acts. And yet they do, says Catherine, if they have no understanding of mercy.

Mercy is all that keeps us from thinking and acting like the world. Many Christian institutions—even churches—are caught up in a business model of life, as opposed to the kingdom values of mercy and compassion. The business world lives by business values, but Christians must live by *kingdom* values—which keep us from becoming enslaved to riches.

Greed, or enslavement to riches, kills the soul, Catherine says. The soul thrives on spiritual food—a life fed by the virtues of charity, mercy, and compassion. Money cannot buy these things, nor can it corrupt them. But the soul enslaved by material things shrivels and dies. Quite simply, we were made for love, mercy, and sharing. We can choose to live otherwise, but we cannot escape the resulting "worm that is always gnawing" at our souls.

Catherine also characterizes the greedy woman as proud and concerned only with her reputation. She lives to look good and keep up with the trends. Her pride and appearance take all her time, and she has no spare time for the needs of others. And despite giving it all her time, the task of keeping up a reputation is never done! She has no time to relax, no peace, no enjoyment of the present. She always has one more purse to buy or another hair color to try, so she never has extra money for missions or hungry children. "Oh, miserable vices that destroy the heaven of the soul!" Catherine laments.

How do I deal with my own greedy desires? I constantly ask myself: Do I *need* this or just *desire* it? How long will it stay in style? Is it more important to me than feeding a child in Sierra Leone?

Generally, just stopping to think is enough reminder to curb my greed. I choose to live a life of kingdom values—and to possess heaven in my soul. ↷

Reflection

1. What things in your life are evidence of greed? What things represent your compassion?

2. In what ways might you take advantage of your neighbors?

3. What does living a life of compassion mean to you? Have you ever thought of greed and compassion as opposites?

4. To what spending habits are you addicted?

5. Do you collect anything that robs others of their daily bread?

Scripture

• Matthew 26:14-16, 47-49
• Matthew 25:31-46
• Matthew 23
• Luke 12:13-21
• Matthew 18:23-35

Exercise

Evaluate your addiction to spending. Refrain from spending money on anything except essentials. Take your lunch. Pass up bargains. How difficult is it for you to resist the lure of consumerism?

The Inn on the Journey

[Catherine hears God speak these words to her.]

Jesus maintains an inn in the Garden of the Holy Church, which keeps and administers the Bread of Life and Blood of the Lamb so that My children, journeying on their pilgrimage, will not faint from weariness along the way. Although you may grow weary, the Body and Blood of My only-begotten Son is available to strengthen you for your journey through this life.

When the weary pilgrim who has passed over the Bridge arrives at the door of this inn, Jesus meets that person, saying, "I am the Way, the Truth, and the Life. Anyone who follows Me does not walk in darkness, but in light." And in another place My Truth [the Bible] says, "No one can come to Me if not through Jesus"—and so indeed it is. Jesus is not only the Inn, but the Road as well. . . . And so Jesus is the Truth, united with Me, the Father. The person who follows this Truth receives the life of grace and cannot faint from hunger because the Truth has become her food. Nor can this person fall in the darkness, because Jesus is light without any falsehood. . . . Therefore, those who follow this road are the sons and daughters of the Truth, because they follow the Truth, and pass through the door of Truth. There, they find themselves united to Me, the Door and the Road and at the same time Infinite Peace.

Both Catherine and I love metaphors. A word picture makes abstract concepts more concrete for me. In this excerpt Catherine explains God's hospitality by envisioning our Lord as an inn. Jesus is the host, meeting weary guests at the door and offering refreshment for body and soul.

I love to travel, especially to Europe. My favorite places to stay are bed-and-breakfasts, where the hosts seem to understand the fullest meaning of comfort and welcome. I prefer a warm, personal atmosphere over the cool sophistication of most hotels. Bed-and-breakfasts offer pleasures like tea, homemade shortbread, and dog-eared novels by the bed. The hosts always seem to give you the scoop on the best local "whatevers" and maps to find them.

Several years ago, Henri Nouwen's book *Reaching Out* forever transformed my concept of hospitality. For Nouwen, hospitality goes far beyond beds and meals—to the concept of making room for guests in your life, not just your home. Nouwen observes that offering yourself to listen, cry with someone, or pray is far harder than making a bed or a meal for an overnight guest. I recommend reading this book for a fuller understanding of hospitality.

Catherine's picture of Jesus as host comes close to Nouwen's understanding of hospitality. Jesus doesn't just own the inn; Jesus *is* the inn. Jesus provides a place for us in his spacious self, which contains rooms labeled Rest, Comfort, Peace, Truth, Grace, and Strength.

Also in this inn we find nourishment. Jesus gives food from his own body and blood. Do we lack spiritual health? Here are all the resources of heaven available to heal our sin-sick souls. Do we struggle to believe in God? Our host offers infinite faith. All we have to do is come and eat from the Bread of life.

Catherine also depicts Jesus as the Road. We come to Jesus by many paths, some well-chosen, some not. But this host provides not only maps but, also in some mystical sense, *is* the road. To come to Jesus is to find the road to truth and life, the road to all the answers we seek. Then, knowing we are on the right road, we can make life's journey in peace.

I have come to understand life as a journey, as opposed to arriving at a series of spiritual goals. Most of us view life as a series of towns along the way to a predetermined destination, which keeps us dissatisfied with our present location and makes us want to push on to the next. But if the journey itself is the goal, then we can appreciate each stop along the way. Our present circumstances have value even though they may not be particularly pleasant. We may not want to prolong our stop here, but our situation will play a part in the overall journey that we can't currently imagine. I have come to believe that life is much more about *process* than *progress*. Particularly if Jesus is the Road, I want to savor the sights along the way.

Catherine assures us that we will not faint from hunger once the Truth has become our food. Nor will we fall in the darkness with Jesus as our light. What does this mean in practical daily terms? Keeping our focus on Jesus and the truths of scripture should guide our decision making. We practice looking to Jesus to meet our needs instead of filling our time with TV and shopping sprees. Jesus will meet our real needs. All the rest are hype from our culture. Choose well on your journey. ∾

Reflection

1. Have you ever thought of your life as a journey? Are you a weary traveler?

2. On what road has your life journey been traveled?

3. What spiritual food do you need from the host, Jesus, today?

4. How does taking Communion feed your soul?

5. In what new direction might Jesus be inviting you?

Scripture

- John 14:6-14
- Isaiah 40:3-5
- Matthew 7:13-14
- Luke 24:13-35
- Luke 10:29-37

Exercise

In your journal, draw the road you have traveled in the last year. Label it and put in the stops along the way.

Now try to imagine where that road might lead. Do you see only one road or perhaps more? Spiritually map out the next few months as you see them now.

Desiring. . .She Sees Me

[Catherine hears God speak these words to her.]

*D*o you know what is special about the blessed ones? They have their desires fulfilled—to see Me. By desiring Me, they possess Me and taste my riches. For they have left the burden of the body, which weighed them down and kept them from a perfect knowledge of the Truth, and prevented them from seeing Me face to face.

But after the soul has left the weight of the body, her [the soul's] desire was fulfilled, for, desiring to see Me, she sees Me, in which vision is her bliss. The soul's vision becomes clear and she knows Me; and in knowing, she loves, and in loving, she tastes Me, Supreme and Eternal Good. And in tasting Me, she is satisfied, and her desire is fulfilled. . . . So you see that My servants are blessed primarily in seeing and in knowing Me—their vision and knowledge are fulfilled. They have tasted what they desired to have, and they are satisfied. . . . In this life, then, they taste the earnest money of eternal life. In tasting this, they will be satisfied.

All of my life beauty has entranced me. I stare at beauty without realizing it: beautiful people, flowers, sunsets, rock formations, seashells, fabric (especially quilts), paintings, snowflakes, and even bugs. I find color especially meaningful. If I have to spend much time in drab surroundings, I feel deprived. Wherever I am, I must have a few colorful items to brighten my surroundings, even if it's only a violet on my desk.

For a long time, I was unaware of this beauty obsession. Then I felt guilty when I realized how much I craved it. I apologized to the Lord, thinking it was worldly of me and unworthy to be so absorbed with creation. After all, shouldn't the Creator deserve more praise than the creation? I felt guilty, but I was unable to wish away my need for beauty. It wasn't simply a preference; it was a need.

Then in the summer of 1994, while in Russia, I

gained an insight from reading a devotional book called *The Lord of the Journey*. This insight not only freed me from my guilt, but also provided a thought that has revolutionized my ideas about all our desires: "The longing to love the beauty of the world in a human being is essentially the longing for the Incarnation."[3] All desires for beauty are a desire for God. God is the creator of beauty, the source of all that is wholesome and good and perfect. My craving for visible beauty was actually a craving to see God.

Suddenly I understood my need to draw that beauty within me and keep it. I actually was longing to partake more and more of my beautiful Christ. The Christ who was present at Creation visited this earth and invested it with ingredients even our dim vision can recognize as godlike.

In today's reading Catherine comments that the "blessed ones" of God are those who are consumed with a desire to see God. The closer we move toward the Creator, the more absorbed we become with the beauty of God's perfection. And we are drawn more and more to the things of God—those things that absorb God's attention. We are being transformed into persons with a godly perspective. I suspect this is the only way we ever see this world clearly—through this "God lens," which the Lord gives us when we desire God more than anything this world offers.

What might it mean to see life from God's perspective? Today's reading gives us one huge clue: We gain an eternal perspective on life.

Phil and I have long practiced a simple test for decision making; we ask ourselves, "Will this have eternal value?" When trying to decide on a course of action and particularly on an expense, we ask, "Will this matter in heaven—or even a month from now?" If it will be of no value in heaven, then it may not be a good use of our time and resources now. This does not rule out enjoying this life or ever spending time or money frivolously, but it often dissipates our desire to squander our resources in light of the needs of people around the world. Giving in to fashion, for example, is a hopeless chase. Fashion is simply about money, and the styles have to change next year to make someone rich. I refuse to be a slave to what is trendy and of no eternal value whatsoever.

But there's an even greater truth for us here. None of these earthly (and temporary) desires ever truly fulfills us. Our heart's desires are satisfied only in desiring, seeing, and knowing God. We chase after many things we think will fulfill us, only to end up disillusioned and even hungrier for something—but we don't know what that something is. Christ is the satisfaction of all desires, not just beauty.

I have come to believe that every desire we experience is really a desire for Christ. Granted, these desires may not be fully satisfied until we reach heaven, but we may experience a "little bit of heaven" in this life if the saints are any indication. Many of them claimed to have heavenly experiences and complete satisfaction of their earthly desires.

We too can experience a little bit of heaven in this life when we desire to see and know God and to live from God's perspective. Catherine summarizes it this way: "It is possible, then, in this life to taste the earnest money of eternal life. In tasting this, they will be satisfied." ⬙

Reflection

1. We all are influenced in many ways—by our families, friends, church, the Bible and other books we read, the entertainment we choose, and so on. Where do you experience the greatest conflict in competing viewpoints?

2. What do you crave? How might this reflect a deeper craving?

3. How often do you think of heaven?

4. What are you chasing instead of God? Why?

5. When have you asked God to meet your deepest desires?

Scripture

- 2 Corinthians 4:7-18
- Revelation 21
- Matthew 6:25-34
- Matthew 7:13-29
- Isaiah 61

Exercise

In your journal, list all your desires, material and spiritual. Then offer them up to the Lord (consider raising your journal upward in a posture of submission). Ask the Lord to grant those desires that are of eternal value. Ask the Lord to meet your heart's desires through true communion with God.

Another Himself

[Catherine hears God speak these words to her.]

*T*he soul, who is lifted by a very great and yearning desire to honor God and be instrumental in the salvation of souls, begins by exercising herself, for a certain amount of time, in the ordinary virtues. She remains in the cell of self-knowledge in order to know better the goodness of God toward her. She does this because knowledge must precede love; for only when the soul has attained love can she strive to follow and clothe herself with the truth. In no way does the creature receive such a taste of the truth, or so brilliant a light therefrom, as by means of humble and continuous prayer, founded on knowledge of herself and God. Prayer, exercising the soul, unites with God the soul that follows the footprints of Christ Crucified. Thus, by desire and affection, and union of love, Christ makes the soul "another Himself." Christ seems to have meant this when he said: "To the one who loves Me and and will observe My commandment, I will reveal Myself. And that person shall be one with Me and I with her. . . . Indeed, through the effect of love, the soul becomes another Himself."

How do we become mirror images of Christ (another Himself)? From Catherine's abstract language, we can identify three steps in this process of being transformed into the likeness of Christ.

The first requirement for becoming images of Christ is a *"very great and yearning desire."* Great desire always precedes transformation, whether it's losing weight or becoming Christlike. I use the word *desire* freely; we desire many things we never expect to possess. For example, I might desire a Mercedes, but it's not likely that I'll ever own one; therefore I do nothing to make that desire a reality. But Catherine's definition of desire more closely resembles discipline.

My spiritual director once told me that discipline is remembering what you really want. Before I eat three cookies, I must keep in mind that I want to lose ten pounds. Otherwise, my desire for the cookies overwhelms my greater desire to lose weight. In this excerpt, on a much larger scale, Catherine refers to desire that is central to who we are and all we do.

What is your "very great and yearning desire"? Practicing Christian virtues is probably not what first comes to mind. But if we truly desire to honor God, practicing scriptural virtues must be such a part of our daily routine that those virtues partially define who we are.

Catherine's second requirement for being this process of becoming "another Himself" is *self-knowledge*. Knowing oneself in order to know God has been a theme for many centuries.

Certainly God knows all about us, but we often hide from truths we do not wish to acknowledge about ourselves. Jung calls it our shadow—the part of ourselves that we hate or ignore but that follows us everywhere. Until we know ourselves fully—both good and repulsive traits—we cannot fully acknowledge how completely God loves us. The Lord loves us totally, all the time, even when we cannot love ourselves.

Therefore, Catherine says, we must dwell in this "cell of self-knowledge" until we understand just how much God loves us. That understanding will transform our lives into a constant song of love and gratitude. Understanding how completely God loves us makes any discipline, any sacrifice seem like nothing. When we have begun to understand ourselves and our worth in God's eyes, we begin to glimpse divine truth and desire to live in it.

Living in truth and honoring God leads to *a life of continual prayer*—an awareness of God's presence and a desire for communication. This is the third requirement for becoming one with God. One right decision leads to another good habit, which becomes a virtue, which ultimately results in transformation.

Many perceive the spiritual life as a mysterious process that is available only to the spiritually elite. Others try to formulate it: Pray like this, and presto—you get your answer to prayer! Catherine says instead that it's all about love.

Let's review the steps to becoming united with God:

1. We begin with a great desire to honor God.
2. We seek self-knowledge and practice virtues.
3. We lead a life of continual prayer.

All of our efforts arise from our love for God. We desire to know and love God wholeheartedly. When that becomes who we are, then we are one with Christ— another Himself. ✍

Reflection

1. What is your great and yearning desire? What are you doing to move toward that desire?

2. How do you desire to honor God? What characteristics of your life might others cite as evidence that you honor God?

3. What spiritual disciplines indicate your devotion to God?

4. How much time do you desire to spend with God daily? How much quality time do you actually spend with your Lord?

5. What areas of self-knowledge have you been avoiding? Why?

Scripture

- 1 Chronicles 29:10-20
- 2 Chronicles 1:7-12
- Psalm 40:1-10
- Psalm 73:23-28
- Matthew 15:3-11

Exercise

Spend some time journaling about your "shadow" qualities. Try to see these areas as parts of yourself that need your love and acceptance. Ask God for feedback about them. Read Psalm 139 to see God's love for *all* of you.

Holy Discernment

[Catherine hears God speak these words to her.]

*M*erit consists in the virtue of love alone, flavored with the light of true discretion [discernment], without which the soul is worth nothing. This love should be directed toward Me endlessly and boundlessly, since I am the Supreme and Eternal Truth. The soul can therefore place neither laws nor limits to her love for Me; but her love for her neighbor, on the contrary, is ordered in certain conditions. . . .

Holy discretion [discernment] ordains that the soul should direct all her powers to My service with zeal, and that she should love her neighbor with such devotion that she would lay down her life for her neighbor a thousand times, if it were possible, . . . enduring pains and torments so that her neighbor may have the life of grace, and giving her temporal substance for the profit and relief of his body. . . .

So you see how discreetly every soul who wishes for grace should pay her debts, that is, should love Me with an infinite love and without measure. But the soul should love her neighbor with measure, with a restricted love, as I have said, not doing herself an injury of sin in order to be useful to others. This is what St. Paul meant when he said that charity ought to be concerned first with self, otherwise it will never be of perfect utility to others. Because when perfection is not in the soul, everything which the soul does for itself and for others is imperfect. It would not, therefore, be just that creatures, who are finite and created by Me, should be saved through offense done to Me, who am the Infinite Good. . . . Therefore in no way should you ever incur the guilt of sin.

And this true love knows well, because she carries with herself the light of holy discretion. This light dispels all darkness, takes away ignorance, and is the companion to every virtue. Holy discretion is a prudence that cannot be deceived, a strength that cannot be beaten, and a perseverance that stretches from heaven to earth. Holy discernment encompasses both knowledge of Me and knowledge of self, love of Me, and love of others.[2]

Discernment ("holy discretion," as Catherine calls it) has become the key element in my spiritual walk. When I pray, I am seeking to discern God's voice. Before I act, I attempt to discern God's will. When I listen to others, I try to discern what they say beneath the words they speak. And even when I listen to myself (praying or journaling), I need to attempt to discern what is going on deep inside.

Phil and I have ministered together for nearly twenty years now, and our ministry has taken us to New Jersey, Pennsylvania, New York, Scotland, Australia, Indiana, and Seattle. Every move required a discernment process. We had to ask ourselves: Where does God want to use us? How can we be sure that we are hearing God's voice correctly? Looking back, I believe that we may have incorrectly discerned only one of those moves—but I say that because of our miserable time in that place. Who knows what God's perspective is on that situation? Perhaps our spiritual growth was the purpose for that year. I certainly have some questions to ask when I get to heaven!

Catherine spends a lot of words on "holy discretion" to emphasize its importance. I found some definitions of *discretion* in an older dictionary that are closer to Catherine's emphasis. *Discretion* is a synonym for prudence and self-control. But the surprising definition that certainly fits her context is this: "the freedom to decide whether to act according to one's own unrestrained will." This reminds us of the impact of loving God and loving others—for we cannot truly love them and still act according to our own unrestrained wills! We must consider the needs of others before our own. To do that, we must stop and reflect (discern) before acting. Most of us need to hone our discernment skills.

Catherine based her thoughts about discernment on the premise that one's life is already surrendered to God. But even the most surrendered Christian experiences turbulence sometimes in trying to discern God's will.

So where does one begin in attempting to discern God's will? Here are some guidelines for discernment that I have found particularly helpful. (I adapted some of these guidelines from Warren Bartlett's ideas, which I heard at a retreat.)

1. *As you pray, imagine the results of a particular course of action.* What are your feelings when you imagine those results—are they peaceful or anxious?

2. *Any decision that is in line with God's will will be confirmed not only by a sense of peace but also a feeling of closeness to God, excitement, and perhaps affirmation by your circumstances.* Consider asking Christian friends and family to pray for discernment with you.

3. *Ask yourself:* How will the kingdom of God benefit from this action?

4. *Do you find yourself eagerly anticipating this new scenario, daydreaming about it, and longing for it?* If so, that is a good sign the decision is in line with God's will. If, on the other hand, you dread it, listen carefully to your own spirit and trust that it is probably not God's will.

5. *Don't assume that God's will is the hardest or least desirable option.* I firmly believe that God fulfills the desires of our hearts when we are surrendered to the Lord, because our desires become the same as God's.

6. *Pay attention to any strange "coincidences" that occur during a discernment period.* Unexpected people or circumstances may reveal God's plan.

7. Another discernment tool Phil and I have used is to *pretend that we have made a decision and to live with it for two weeks.* We pay attention to how the decision makes us feel, what happens during our times of prayer, and even the dreams we have during that time. Then we reverse our decision and live with it for two weeks. This test usually results in obvious discernment of a right direction and a wrong one. (This suggestion comes from *Inviting the Mystic, Supporting the Prophet* by Katherine Marie Dyckman and L. Patrick Carroll.)

8. *Follow any promptings to particular passages of scripture during a discernment time.* If you feel drawn to a passage, read it slowly and meditatively and ask the Lord to speak through it. You may not always get a yes or no answer to your decision, but God may reveal a message to you through the passage.

Prayer and discernment are never a formula, but we can learn to listen and reflect more closely—taking time to notice the movement of the Spirit in us through the above means. Catherine would be the first to agree that discernment is not a gimmick, but it can and must be cultivated if we want to be God's women. For, as she says, holy discernment is a light that "dispels all darkness, takes away all ignorance, and is the companion to every virtue." ❧

Reflection

1. How do you normally discern God's will? What process has worked for you in the past?

2. How has your practice of discernment changed over your years of walking with the Lord?

3. Have you ever tried a group discernment experience, inviting others to pray with you as you seek God's direction for your life?

4. What would you very much like to discern about your life right now? How have you been approaching this process?

5. How does discernment in your life affect the lives of those around you?

Scripture

• Philippians 1:6-20
• Proverbs 3:13-26
• Psalm 37:1-11
• Isaiah 30:21; 48:16-19
• Deuteronomy 10:12-22

Exercise

Choose one or more of the above suggestions for discernment and apply it/them to some area of your life where you seek God's direction. Note your inner responses in your journal.

$\mathcal{N}otes$

NOTES ON THE TEXT

1. *A Life of Total Prayer: Selected Writings of Catherine of Siena*, Upper Room Spiritual Classics, ed. Keith Beasley-Topliffe (Nashville, Tenn.: Upper Room Books, 2000), 68–69.

TERESA OF ÁVILA

1. Teresa of Avila, *Interior Castle*, translated and edited by E. Allison Peers (New York: Image Books, 1961), 28–33.

2. Tom Sine, *Mustard Seed vs. McWorld: Reinventing Life and Faith for the Future* (Grand Rapids, Mich.: Baker Book House, 1999), 92.

3. *Interior Castle*, 46–50.

4. Ibid., 65–67.

5. C. S. Lewis, *The Last Battle* (New York: Collier Books, 1970), 154.

6. *Interior Castle*, 72–77.

7. Philip Schaff, ed., *A Select Library of the Nicene and Post-Nicene Fathers of the Christian Church*, vol. 7 (Grand Rapids, Mich.: Wm. B. Eerdmans Publishing Company, 1956), 504.

8. *Interior Castle*, 104–06.

9. From a letter to Don Lorenzo de Cepeda (Teresa's brother), January 17, 1577, *The Letters of Saint Teresa of Jesus*, edited and translated by E. Allison Peers (London: Burns Oates & Washbourne, Ltd., 1951), 410.

10. From a letter to her brother, January 17, 1577, Peers, *The Letters of Saint Teresa of Jesus*, 412.

11. From a letter to her brother, February 27–28, 1577, Peers, 436.

12. From a letter to her brother, February 10, 1577, Peers, 430.

13. From a letter to her brother, January 17, 1577, Peers, 410–11.

14. *Interior Castle*, 37–38.

15. *The Life of Teresa of Jesus*, edited and translated by E. Allison Peers (New York: Image Books, 1960), 127–29.

16. Ibid., 148–49.

17. Ibid., 163–64.

18. Ibid., 174, 177.

19. Ibid., 149.

20. *Interior Castle*, 129, 135, 138–41, 149–50.

21. *New Catholic Encyclopedia*, s.v. "locutions."

Madame Jeanne Guyon

1. *The Works of John Wesley*, vol. 14 (Grand Rapids, Mich.: Zondervan, n.d.), 278.
2. Jeanne Guyon, *Experiencing the Depths of Jesus Christ* (Nashville, Tenn.: Thomas Nelson Publishers, 2000), 37–39.
3. Ibid., 1, 3–4.
4. Ibid., 7–8.
5. Ibid., 107–08.
6. Ibid., 101–02.
7. Ibid., 22–24.
8. Ibid., 16, 18–19.
9. Ibid., 11–13.
10. Ibid., 27–29.
11. From "In the Garden," C. Austin Miles, 1913.
12. *Experiencing the Depths of Jesus Christ*, 37–38.
13. Ibid., 132–33.

Thérèse of Lisieux

1. *Autobiography of a Saint:Thérèse of Lisieux*, trans. by Ronald Knox (London: The Harville Press, 1958), 187.
2. Ibid., 249.
3. *Autobiography of St. Thérèse of Lisieux*, trans. by Ronald Knox (New York: P. J. Kenedy and Sons, 1958), 34–35.
4. Ibid., 36–37.
5. Ibid., 262–63.
6. From "Trust and Obey," John H. Sammis, 1887 (based on 1 John 1:7).
7. *Autobiography of Saint Thérèse of Lisieux*, 105–06.
8. Ibid., 181.
9. *Autobiography of a Saint*, 269.
10. *Autobiography of St. Thérèse of Lisieux*, 142.
11. Ibid., 198.
12. Bruce Demarest, *Satisfy Your Soul* (Colorado Springs, Colo.: NavPress, 1999), 214.
13. *Autobiography of Saint Thérèse of Lisieux*, 171.
14. Ibid., 280.

Julian of Norwich

1. Adapted from Julian, Anchoress at Norwich, *Revelations of Divine Love* (London: Methuen & Company, 1901), 10.

2. Ibid., 202–03.
3. Ibid., 34–35.
4. C. S. Lewis, *A Grief Observed* (New York: Bantam Books, 1976), 4.
5. Adapted from *Revelations of Divine Love*, 33–34.
6. Ibid., 80–81.
7. *A Select Library of the Nicene and Post-Nicene Fathers of the Christian Church*, vol. 1, Philip Schaff, ed. (Grand Rapids, Mich.: Wm. B. Eerdmans Publishing Company, 1956), 152.
8. Adapted from *Revelations of Divine Love*, 101–02.
9. Ibid., 3–5.
10. Ibid., 24–25.
11. Ibid., 58–59.
12. Ibid., 61.
13. Ibid., 10.
14. Ibid., 144–45.

Catherine of Siena

1. All excerpts from *The Dialogue of Saint Catherine of Siena* are taken from the following Web site: http: //ccel.org/c/catherine/dialog/dialog1.0.html.
2. Paul Tillich, *The Shaking of the Foundations* (New York: Charles Scribner's Sons, 1948), 161–62.
3. Simone Weil, quoted in *The Lord of the Journey: A Reader in Christian Spirituality*, edited and compiled by Roger Pooley and Philip Seddon (London: Collins Liturgical Publications, 1986), 60.

Suggested Reading

Editor's Note: Many editions of the classic works are available in libraries and book stores.

Bouyer, Louis. *Women Mystics: Hadewijch of Antwerp, Teresa of Ávila, Thérèse of Lisieux, Elizabeth of the Trinity, and Edith Stein.* Trans. Ann E. Nash. San Francisco, Calif: Ignatius Press, 1993. Includes background and excerpts from the five mystics.

Catherine of Siena. *The Dialogue of the Seraphic Virgin.* Translated from the original Italian, with an introduction on the life and times of the saint by Algar Thorold. London: Kegan Paul, Trench, Trubner & Co. Ltd., 1906. Web site: www.ccel.org/c/catherine/dialog/dialog.html

———. *The Dialogue.* Trans. Suzanne Noffke. New York: Paulist Press, 1980.

De Sola Chervin, Ronda. *Prayers of the Women Mystics.* Ann Arbor, Mich.: Servant Publications, 1992. Includes Catherine of Siena, Hildegard of Bingen, Julian of Norwich, Joan of Arc, Teresa of Ávila, and fourteen other mystics.

Demarest, Bruce. *Satisfy Your Soul.* Colorado Springs, Colo.: NavPress Publishing Group, 1999.

Durka, Gloria. *Praying with Julian of Norwich.* Companions for the Journey Series. Winona, Minn.: Saint Mary's Press, 1989.

Dyckman, Katherine Marie and L. Patrick Carroll. *Inviting the Mystic, Supporting the Prophet.* New York: Paulist Press, 1981.

Farmer, David Hugh. *The Oxford Dictionary of Saints.* 4th ed. New York: Oxford University Press, 1997.

Fleming, David A., ed. *The Fire and the Cloud: An Anthology of Catholic Spirituality*. New York: Paulist Press, 1978.

Flinders, Carol Lee. *Enduring Grace: Living Portraits of Seven Women Mystics*. San Francisco, Calif.: HarperSan Francisco, 1993. Biographical information on Clare of Assisi, Mechthild of Magdeburg, Julian of Norwich, Catherine of Siena, Catherine of Genoa, Teresa of Ávila, and Thérèse of Lisieux.

Grant, Patrick, ed. *A Dazzling Darkness: An Anthology of Western Mysticism*. Grand Rapids, Mich.: W. B. Eerdmans Publishing Co., 1985. Short quotations from eighty-five men and women saints through the centuries.

Guyon, Madame. *Experiencing the Depths of Jesus Christ*. Nashville, Tenn.: Thomas Nelson, 2000.

Saint Hildegard. *Secrets of God: Writings of Hildegard of Bingen*. Trans. Sabina Flanagan. Boston, Mass.: Shambhala, 1996.

Julian of Norwich. *I Promise You a Crown*. Ed. David Hazzard. Minneapolis, Minn.: Bethany House, 1995.

———. *Revelations of Divine Love*. Harrisburg, Pa.: Morehouse Publishing, 2000.

Kempe, Margery. *The Book of Margery Kempe*. New York: W. W. Norton & Co., 2001. Margery was a contemporary and protégée of Julian of Norwich.

Nouwen, Henri J. M. *Gracias!: A Latin American Journal*. Maryknoll, N.Y.: Orbis Books, 1993.

———. *Reaching Out: The Three Movements of the Spiritual Life*. New York: Image Books, 1986.

Pooley, Roger and Philip Seddon, eds. *The Lord of the Journey: A Reader in Christian Spirituality*. San Francisco, Calif.: Collins, 1986.

Schmidt, Joseph F. *Praying with Thérèse of Lisieux*. Companions for the Journey Series. Winona, Minn: Saint Mary's Press, 1992.

Silf, Margaret. *Inner Compass: An Invitation to Ignatian Spirituality*. Chicago, Ill.: Loyola Press, 1999.

Teresa of Ávila. *Interior Castle: or The Mansions*. Edited by Father Benedict Zimmerman and translated by Benedictines of Stanbrook Staff. Rockford, Ill.: TAN Books and Publishers, 1997.

———. *The Life of Teresa of Jesus*. Translated and edited by E. Allison Peers. New York: Image Books, 1991.

———. *The Autobiography of Saint Teresa of Ávila: Including the Revelations*. Trans. David Lewis. Rockford, Ill.: TAN Books and Publishers, 1997.

Thérèse of Lisieux. *Autobiography of Saint Thérèse of Lisieux*. New York: P. J. Kenedy & Sons, 1958.

Thérèse of Lisieux. *Prayers and Meditations of Thérèse of Lisieux*. Edited by Cindy Cavnar. Ann Arbor, Mich.: Servant Publications, 1993.

Web Sites

See www.ccel.org/index/classics.html for an index of Christian classics (listed by author in alphabetical order).

About the Author

Kathy Bence is a minister, writer, and spiritual director who lives in Seattle, Washington. She is working toward a Doctor of Ministry in Spiritual Formation degree at Azusa Pacific University in Los Angeles and hopes to develop a retreat/spiritual direction ministry. She and her husband, Phil, are also adjunct professors at the Seattle branch of Fuller Seminary.

Kathy and Phil have twenty years of ministry experience in pastoring, missions, and teaching theology at the college level.

Kathy's previous books include *Turn Off the TV* (Zondervan) and *Developing Christian Values* (Standard Publishing). She has also written numerous articles for *Today's Christian Woman* magazine. Kathy is an ordained clergywoman in the Wesleyan Church. She and Phil attend St. Alban's Episcopal Church in Edmonds, Washington.

THE UPPER ROOM SPIRITUAL CLASSICS®

compiled and introduced by Keith Beasley-Topliffe

Every book in each set of *The Upper Room Spiritual Classics®* contains introductory material, writer biographical information, 14 reader-friendly selections from the writer, and a study guide in the appendix. *The Upper Room Spiritual Classics®* will help both individuals and study groups grow in the faith by seeing God through the eyes of remarkable spiritual leaders.

The Upper Room Spiritual Classics®, Series 1

For those of us eager to deepen our spiritual lives through the great devotional writings of the church, Upper Room Books® presents readable translations of five writers — John Wesley, Thomas Kelly, John Cassian, Teresa of Avila, and Augustine.

The series offers a deeper understanding of prayer, insights into approaching and knowing God, and support for growth in the spiritual life. Also included in each volume is an appendix on how to read the devotional writings fruitfully and how to apply the writers' spiritual insights to your daily life.

#832 $24.00 (Boxed set, 5 titles in slipcase)

Titles in Series 1

- *A Longing for Holiness: Selected Writings of John Wesley*
  #827 $5.00
- *The Soul's Passion for God: Selected Writings of Teresa of Avila*
  #828 $5.00
- *The Sanctuary of the Soul: Selected Writings of Thomas Kelly*
  #829 $5.00
- *Hungering for God: Selected Writings of Augustine*
  #830 $5.00
- *Making Life a Prayer: Selected Writings of John Cassian*
  #831 $5.00

The Upper Room Spiritual Classics®, Serie

With this second set of devotional classics, Upper Room Books offers selections from more great Christian writers — Francis and Clare, Julian of Norwich, Evelyn Underhill, Toyohiko Kagawa, and Thomas à Kempis.

#853 $24.00 (Boxed set, 5 titles in slipcase)

Titles in Series 2

- *Encounter with God's Love: Selected Writings of Julian of Norwich*
  #833 $5.00
- *The Riches of Simplicity: Selected Writings of Francis and Clare*
  #834 $5.00
- *A Pattern for Life: Selected Writings of Thomas à Kempis*
  #835 $5.00
- *The Soul's Delight: Selected Writings of Evelyn Underhill*
  #837 $5.00
- *Living Out Christ's Love: Selected Writings of Toyohiko Kagawa*
  #836 $5.00

The Upper Room Spiritual Classics®, Series 3

This third set of devotional classics includes wisdom from spiritual leaders who strove to devote their lives totally to the will of God: John of the Cross, the Desert Fathers and Mothers, John Law, John Woolman, and Catherine of Siena. The stories and writings of these devotional leaders can inspire and guide believers today as they have for centuries.

#905 $24.00 (Boxed set, 5 titles in slipcase)

Titles in Series 3

- *Loving God Through the Darkness: Selected Writings of John of the Cross*
  #904 $5.00
- *Seeking a Purer Christian Life: The Desert Mothers and Fathers*
  #902 $5.00
- *Total Devotion to God: Selected Writings of William Law*
  #901 $5.00
- *Walking Humbly with God: Selected Writings of John Woolman*
  #900 $5.00
- *A Life of Total Prayer: Selected Writings of Catherine of Siena*
  #903 $5.00